THE INSIDER'S GUIDE TO CONSULTING SUCCESS

INSIGHTS AND ADVICE FROM AN INDUSTRY INSIDER

How to establish, operate and grow a consulting practice

Edward D. Hendricks

MACMILLAN SPECTRUM

An imprint of MACMILLAN • USA

A Simon & Schuster Macmillan Company

1633 Broadway

New York, NY 10019-6785

A Spectrum Book

MACMILLAN and SPECTRUM are registered trademarks of Macmillan, Inc.

Library of Congress Cataloging-in-Publication Data

Macmillan Publishing books may be purchased for busiess or sales promotional use. For information please write: Special Markets Department, Macmillan Publishing USA, 1633 Broadway, New York, NY 10019.

Hendricks, Edward

Cataloging-in-Publication data available upon request from the Library of Congress.

ISBN 0-02-861540-9

Manufactured in the United States of America

10 9 8 7 6 5 4 3 2 1

Book Design by Margaret Dubois

Neither the persons quoted nor the organizations referred to in this book have authorized or endorsed the content of this book or any particular concept, proposition, or conclusion set forth in it. All quotations used and references made herein are strictly for purposes of illustration.

Although this Guide isn't designed to address issues dealing with doing business outside the United States, if you are intending to do so you should consult with your tax lawyer, your business lawyer, and your insurance and account-ing advisors on credit issues, your company's warranty coverage, distributor agreements, insurance coverages, and related topics appropriate to your particular company.

CONTENTS

ACKNOWLEDGMENTS

Consulting is far too broad an industry and topic to be covered thoroughly in any single book. In fact, some MBA programs (such as at New York University's Stern School) offer a concentration in Consulting for MBA students and even then just barely scratch the surface. Therefore, this book does not purport to have all the answers, or even all the questions. What this book does do is provide an opportunity for the reader to look at some of the issues faced by consulting firms, and how some of the more successful firms have learned to deal with them. The observations contained in this book are my own, and I will not attempt to blame anyone else for them.

But I would not be in a position to make the observations at all had it not been for several people whose faith in me allowed me to get on the inside so I could write *An Insider's Guide*. My heartfelt thanks to Joseph J. Brady who preceded me as President of ACME—the association of management consulting firms—and who hired me to work at the association all those years ago. And to James H. Kennedy, Publisher of *Consultants News* and watchdog of the ethics and professionalism of consulting firms and consulting practitioners who encouraged me and kept me on my toes.

Thanks, also to Dudly Smith and Mary-Bridget Klinkenbergh, who presently run ACME, for their many kindnesses and willingness to let me quote so freely from many of ACME's publications.

A very sincere thank you goes to Dick Staron, my editor at Macmillan for his savvy and support and who kept pushing me to succeed. Thanks as well to Ford Harding of Harding & Company who introduced me to Dick Staron in the first place, and to the other members of my networking group: John Bliss, Terry Gallagher, Dallas Kersey, and Chuck Goldberg, each of whom is a successful consultant in his own right.

And finally, from the bottom of my heart, thanks to the person without whom this book would never have been written, my strongest supporter, my collaborator, my typist, my wife—Betty—who never lost faith even when the going got tough with the cyclicality of the consulting business.

If this book is a help to you at all, it is because of the willingness of my clients to share their own experiences and to help me understand what it really takes to succeed.

INTRODUCTION

WHO THIS BOOK IS FOR

The Insider's Guide To Consulting Success is written for people who are considering a career in consulting, as well as for those who have up-and-running firms which they want to grow into larger firms. It's loaded with advice and help in solving real-world problems.

You're stuck in a dead-end job and crave diversity and creativity in your life. Your present employer is downsizing, and you've been offered early retirement, but you're too young (or broke, or both) to really retire. You're good at giving advice and solving problems, so all of your friends are telling you that you should be a consultant.

Or, maybe you've already made the transition and have set up a consulting practice. Now you're worried about making it grow (or even simply survive). You're thinking about succession planning and merger and acquisition issues. You want to compete more successfully or enter new markets, while still maintaining strong relationships with your clients.

Where do you find help in making these decisions or dealing with these issues?

Right here in this *Insider's Guide,* which is based on the practical experience and insights I've gained in running an international trade association of management consulting firms, lecturing and teaching consulting courses at universities and graduate schools, and as a consultant to consulting firms. When it comes to consulting, I've "been there, done that." That's what makes this an *Insider's Guide.*

Whether you're just beginning to explore the consulting field, are a new entrant or a wizened veteran, this book will be of interest to you. The suggestions and insights are not limited to only my own experiences, or even the way a single firm would address them. This book is packed with ideas gleaned from a variety of sources to help *you* succeed.

Running a consulting practice is a lot easier if you have a "friendly co-pilot" or mentor to help you identify opportunities and navigate around problem areas. This *Insider's Guide* is like having an old friend in the business who is willing to share information with you in a clear-cut, plain-English manner without resorting to academic gobbledy-gook or "consultantese." This book has been written for *you,* and you don't have time for a lot of extraneous words or esoteric theories.

Before moving on, let me share a little about myself and the genesis of this *Insider's Guide*.

"Tell me, again, exactly what is it that you do?" I wish I had a nickel for each time I heard that question from my father over the past twenty years that I have been involved in the field of consulting. And no matter how many different ways I tried to describe what a consultant does, each new project would result in my having to rethink my answer and expand upon my previous attempts at giving a comprehensive definition. Eventually I would simply say, "I'm a management consultant. I help companies solve problems and take advantage of opportunities." My father may not have been totally satisfied, but it was the best I could come up with on short notice.

Then, to make attempts to describe what I did even more difficult, in 1979 I joined that staff of ACME—the international association of management consulting firms. (ACME was formerly known as the *Association of Consulting Management Engineers* when it was founded in 1929, so, yes at one time the acronym did fit the name. But that's another story.) Now I was not only a consultant, but I was an association executive as well! It may have been hard to describe, but it placed me in the unique position of being a consultant to consulting firms, as well as providing me with a bird's eye view of the global world of consulting. It also afforded me insights as to what prospective clients were looking for when they wanted to hire consultants, as well as an opportunity to watch consulting firms and to learn why some are so successful while others seem to struggle.

This book is an attempt to share what I have learned as an "insider" about some of the factors contributing to that success.

CLIENT-SAVVY CONSULTING

> *Understanding what clients really want and responding to their needs are crucial factors in consulting success.*

The Insider's Guide is designed to help you expand your consulting practice and make it more profitable. The key to doing that is to understand and apply *client-savvy*.

To understand the concept of *client-savvy* you need to do a couple of things, including looking outside of yourself and your firm to focus on what the client is saying, what he/she wants today, and to anticipate what his/her needs will be tomorrow.

1. First, you have to put yourself into your client's mind, to view the world and his/her situation from his/her perspective. You've got to understand how the client is interpreting the problem if you really want to help the client accomplish the *change* necessary to solve the problem.

Understanding where the client is coming from is the basis for building a relationship with that client. And success in consulting is directly correlated to the strength of the relationship you have with your clients.

When you get right down to it, the core of consulting is people skills. The client may want a new computer system installed, but he/she hires *people* to accomplish the installation.

2. Second, as a consultant you are expected not only to help the client solve the problem he/she is facing today, but to also help the client anticipate future problems and opportunities.

Client-savvy means that you are going to have to be forward-thinking and not just reactionary. You are going to have to pay attention and be able to interpret trends in the world at large and not just in the industry or functional area in which you specialize. Your clients can usually track changes in their industry; they expect more from their consultant than to tell them what they already know.

Problem-Solver 1-1
BECOMING CLIENT-SAVVY

The Issue

How can *The Insider's Guide to Consulting Success* help me to become more client-savvy?

Let's Work This Through

We learn from experience, either by being involved in the event ourselves, or by having someone else share their experience with us.

The *Insider's Guide* lets you in on what clients are looking for when they want to hire consultants, and what consultants have done that have helped them to respond successfully to the needs of clients.

The information in this book can get you in touch with the way clients think, and by thus being fore-armed, you will enhance the likelihood that you, too, can be more successful.

Client-savvy involves looking at your consulting practice and the services you offer from the perspective of the client. It is more than simply thinking like a client, but getting inside the client's head and *becoming* this other person. You've got to address the inner needs of the client, not just what he/she says he/she wants. Once you can demonstrate that you can provide a prospective client with the *benefits* he is looking for and are not just offering features, the assignment will be yours.

HOW CLIENT-SAVVY WORKS

Client-savvy is the ability to see your consulting practice from the mind of the client and to understand the client's present problem and to anticipate future issues and needs.

The key to successful consulting engagements rests on the strength of the relationship between the consultant and the client. Relationships in turn are based on understanding, trust, and respect. The success of consulting projects is not just measured in numbers, but also on the way the client *feels* about the experience of having worked with the consultant.

To help ensure the success of their projects, client-savvy consultants realize that not only must they understand their clients, but the client must likewise understand the consultant. You will want to make sure that you and all of the employees of your consulting firm are sending out the right signals and messages, and that they are being sent out clearly.

For example, you want to make the client feel that it is easy to do business with you. This perception starts with the way your telephone is answered from the operator, through your assistant, to you. If at any point in the telephone chain the client receives or perceives a conflicting message about your firm's commitment to service and customer relationships, you will be hard-pressed to recapture the client's good graces. You can't blame being short-tempered or inconsiderate on being under pressure—the client has hired you to relieve some of the pressure he/she is facing.

As a consultant, people are going to expect a lot out of you. You have to manage those expectations. Never promise more than you can deliver. Instead, deliver more than you promise. People appreciate pleasant surprises; they hate being disappointed. Your success in consulting will be measured against what your clients were expecting.

But client-savvy involves more than both managing expectations and understanding and dealing with people. It also includes the ability to be aware of and solve current problems, plus anticipating future concerns. Thus, client-savvy consulting is actually a combination of interrelated skills rather than any one single attribute. Successful, client-savvy consultants are able to:

▲ Get into the minds of their clients and prospective clients to understand what they really want and need and then *respond* to those driving forces.

▲ Manage diverse, and often conflicting, expectations from a variety of sources.

▲ Understand and solve specific problems while not losing sight of the "big picture" of the client organization as a system, as well of the external world in which it operates.

▲ Visualize and anticipate future problems, trends, and scenarios and assess their impact on the client organization, the consulting firm itself, and on the competition—both of the client and the consultant.

Problem-Solver 1-2
CONSULTING IS A PEOPLE BUSINESS

The Issue

Consulting would be a great job if only you didn't have to deal with people, both clients and your own staff.

Let's Work This Through

It shouldn't and doesn't have to feel like running a consulting practice involves constant problems with people. Take the time to understand what the people you deal with really want, and then find ways to place everyone in win-win situations as often as possible:

1. Clients want your help in solving their problems. They are willing to pay a reasonable amount for this assistance; but they want to get their money's worth. The results of many consulting projects are hard to empirically measure, so you must make the client "feel" good about his/her experience with your firm and, therefore, feel your fees are justified.

2. Your employees want to work on interesting and diverse projects to gain experience, but clients don't want to provide "on the job training" for consultants. You need to find ways to develop balanced work teams of new and experienced consultants, while still maintaining the leverage needed to be profitable.

3. Your clients expect you and your staff to be available whenever and wherever the client asks them to be. Meanwhile, your employees are demanding more balanced lifestyles. You may have to do some creative juggling and time management in order to keep most people somewhat happy.

There's no doubt about it, consulting is a people business. You can't hide behind numbers or technology.

Problem-Solver I-3

TOMORROW'S SUCCESS BEGINS TODAY

The Issue

I've got so many decisions to make and things to do today, how can I handle it all and worry about the future?

Let's Work This Through

The answer is: Everything you do today should be based on your beliefs of what you *want* the future to be.

The future belongs to those who create the future they want.

▲ Anticipate your client's needs and have new products and services ready to go before clients begin to ask for them.

▲ Anticipate your staffing needs *and* the needs of your staff. Roller coasters belong in amusement parks, not in your HR practices.

▲ Anticipate what your competitors are likely to do and *who* your competitors are likely to be.

Project yourself into the future and visualize yourself and your firm as successful, and start today to act as if you had already reached that goal. Remember, in business and in life, you tend to get what you expect to get.

When all is said and done, your success in consulting depends on you and your ability to manage:

▲ People—employees, clients, competitors—and their expectations.

▲ Money—both income and costs.

▲ Yourself—your time, focus, motivation, health, etc

THE INSIDER'S GUIDE

An Insider's Guide To Success In Consulting does not purport to be the definitive resource that will answer all of everyone's questions about the field of consulting. It will, however, answer some questions and should be a help to those readers who are considering whether they should enter the field of consulting or not. It is also designed to be of use to those who are already in the field and are interested in growing their businesses. I have tried to make this book both useful and easy to read. You will have to be the judge as to whether I have succeeded in reaching these goals.

Consulting is not for everyone. It requires hard work, energy, enthusiasm, business acumen, and interpersonal skills far in excess of those needed to succeed in most other ways of earning a living. For those with the requisite abilities, however, it can be tremendously fulfilling, because as a consultant you truly can make a difference. And when you get right down to it, isn't that what life is all about—to have made a positive difference because you have lived?

1
AN OVERVIEW

CONSULTING—A GROWING BUSINESS

For corporations around the globe, the 1990s have been an era of transformation. Technological advances, alternative compensation schemes, fierce competition driving cost-cutting programs and a raft of initial-laden techniques such as JIT and TQM leading to the euphemism of the month club with such terms as "downsizing," "rightsizing," "outsourcing," and "entrapreneurship," and even "inter"- and "intrapreneurship" are now entering our everyday vocabulary. It is no wonder that CEOs, COOs, CIOs, and all levels of company management are turning more and more frequently to outside experts to analyze business problems, to help them make sense out of chaos, and even to perform tasks that used to be handled in-house. We are undoubtedly in the midst of unprecedented change, and as change agents, consulting firms are booming.

Management consulting has long been recognized as one of the fastest growing industries. Recent research conducted by ACME—the association of management consulting firms—shows that in 1995 management consulting firms experienced fee growth of nearly 18%, nearly **nine times** the growth rate of the GDP in that year.[1] And this was not an unusual occurrence. In the five-year period between 1990–1995, the average annual consulting fee growth rate in the United States was 13%.[2] It is hardly surprising that various pundits have called the 90s "The Decade of the Consultant."

Because consulting is an unregulated business, it is not possible to gather completely accurate figures as to how many consultants there are or how big the market really is. James H. Kennedy, publisher of *Consultants News*[3], a trade newsletter, each year releases estimates about the size of the profession.

Problem Solver 1-1
CONSULTING IS GROWING

The Issue

Why is the consulting business growing?

Let's Work This Through

1. There is little doubt that the rate of change is increasing in the business world. It is not unusual today to witness whole companies and even entire industries being reshaped with the resultant upheaval leading managers of those companies to seek advice from consultants with the experience they themselves lack.

2. Stockholders of companies today are demanding more and in ever shorter timeframes. Managers perceive that they no longer have time to reflect on the impact of change or to learn new styles and techniques for dealing with it. Consultants are brought in to "jump-start" new management techniques.

3. Technology continues to shrink distance and time. It truly has become a global market-place, and only those firms with up-to-date technological capabilities are going to compete successfully. However, keeping up with change in technology is beyond the in-house ability of many client organizations, so they often turn to consultants to bring them the specialized advice they need.

4. Knowledge itself has become a competitive necessity. Companies need to know about and how to implement the "best practices" used by other firms from different industries. This requires a broader perspective than most clients have, so again, they rely on the broad experience of consulting firms.

Jim divides management consulting into two distinct segments: advice and counsel, and everything else (e.g., information technology and implementation). For 1995 he breaks the revenues of the industry down as follows:

	Advice & Counsel	All Management Consulting
United States	$21B	$43B
Worldwide	$40B	$83B

Estimates are that there are some 140,000 management consultants practicing full time in the U.S. and about 250,000 full-time management consultants worldwide. Now, if the revenues were divided evenly, each consultant would be doing quite nice-ly. But there is considerable disparity in the distribution of the revenues. For example, the 40 largest U.S.-based management consulting firms accounted for over 50% of all billings. The revenues of the top 100 firms make up nearly ¾ of the entire market, leaving the remaining 25% to be divided among hundreds of firms and thousands of individual practitioners. Management consulting is a competitive business, and the playing field is not always even.

A listing of the 40 largest U.S.-based management consulting firms is as follows:

40 LARGEST U.S.-BASED MANAGEMENT CONSULTING FIRMS
(According to Consultants News)[4]

1.	Andersen Consulting	21.	Milliman & Robertson
2.	McKinsey & Co.	22.	CSC Consulting Group
3.	Ernst & Young	23.	Grant Thornton
4.	Arthur Andersen	24.	The Hay Group
5.	KMPG Peat Marwick	25.	Sedgwick Noble Lowndes
6.	Coopers & Lybrand Consulting	26.	Buck Consultants
7.	Deloitte & Touche	27.	A. Foster Higgins & Co.
8.	Mercer Consulting Group	28.	Alexander Consulting Group
9.	Towers Perrin	29.	Godwins International
10.	Booz-Allen & Hamilton	30.	Monitor Company
11.	A.T. Kearney	31.	Proudfoot
12.	IBM Consulting Group	32.	George S. May International
13.	Watson Wyatt Worldwide	33.	The Segal Company
14.	The Boston Consulting Group	34.	ICF Kaiser International
15.	Gemini Consulting	35.	Kurt Salmon Associates
16.	Hewitt Associates	36.	McGladry & Pullen
17.	Price Waterhouse	37.	AT&T Solutions
18.	Bain & Company	38.	Marakon Associates
19.	Arthur D. Little	39.	Strategic Decisions Group
20.	American Management Systems	40.	First Manhattan Consulting Group

Just as some firms do better than others, so too are some practice areas growing more rapidly than others. Likewise, recent data indicates that larger assignments are being awarded more frequently which, in turn, contributes to the higher rate of growth for the bigger firms. The data below is from a survey conducted by the trade association of management consulting firms and highlights some of the differences in growth rates.

1995 MEDIAN CONSULTING FEE GROWTH BY CONSULTING SPECIALTY
1996 ACME Survey of U.S. Key Management Information[5]

Consulting Specialty	1995 Median Fee Growth
Health Care Consulting	13.5%
Human Resources	15.1%
Production Management	38.7%
Strategic Planning	14.6%
Other Specializations	25.7%
No Specialty	8.1%

The size of the firm, too, makes a difference, with larger firms growing faster than smaller firms as evidenced from ACME's research as presented below.

Annual Consulting Fees	Growth
Less than $1,000,000	15.1%
$1–$4 Million	15.0%
$4–$25 Million	18.4%
More than $25 Million	21.3%

CHARACTERISTICS OF MANAGEMENT CONSULTING

Based on definitions offered by such organizations as ACME, the U.S. Institute of Management Consultants, and the Institute of Management Consultants in the United Kingdom, we begin to see certain commonalities that may help to bring the role of consultants into a clearer focus.

First is an emphasis on *independence*. To be effective, a consultant must be allowed to function with *objectivity*. The consultant is not an employee of the client organization and must be free to gather and interpret data and information based on his or her own experience, and not automatically accept the views of the client. This means that the consultant has an obligation to determine the extent or nature of the client's

---

Problem-Solver 1-2
DEFINING MANAGEMENT CONSULTING

The Issue

Is there a concise definition of consulting?

Let's Work This Through

Everybody talks about consulting and management consulting, but there is no one, universally accepted definition. However, ACME offers the following:

▲ Management consulting is a service performed for a fee by independent, objective professionals to help managers define and achieve their organization's goals.

▲ By analyzing problems or opportunities associated with key management functions, management consultants can recommend practical solutions and help to implement them.

▲ In simplest terms, management consulting is the business of managing change, and management consultants are skilled, knowledgeable agents of change.

▲ The ultimate purpose of every consulting engagement is to make something happen in the client organization that will improve its performance.

▲ Change for the better is the ultimate measure of success.

---

actual problem and not necessarily rely on the client's diagnosis. The consultant must be free to disagree with the client when necessary, and the most successful assignments are characterized by more of a partnership arrangement between the client and consultant than a master/servant relationship. The consultant also brings a fresh *perspective* to solving the client's problem. Based on an ability to step back and view the issues from outside the organization, combined with the experience of having helped other companies address similar concerns, the consultant can recommend solutions the client may not have thought of. Thus the consultant can formulate a separate appraisal of the problem and recommend alternative solutions that are in the client's best interests.

Second is a realization that management consultants provide *advice* to managers of client organizations. They do not make the ultimate decision as to whether the client organization will implement their recommendations, and clients must be careful not to abdicate their responsibility by giving too much authority to consultants. As advisors, consultants have an obligation to the client for the quality, integrity, and timeliness of the advice, and for presenting it in such a manner that it is most helpful to the client. But it remains with the client to decide whether or not to take or to use that advice. This does not mean, however, that consultants cannot or should not be asked to assist in implementing solutions. After all, it does not usually make sense to bring in a change agent/consultant to perpetuate doing the same things in the same way.

Third is an awareness that consultants bring *specialized knowledge and professional skills* to bear in addressing the client's needs. True management consultants, in the full sense of the term, have accumulated considerable knowledge of different management situations and have developed strong skills in interpersonal communications, as well as abilities in identifying problems, analyzing information, selecting alternative courses of action, etc. Professional management consultants are not "executives between jobs;" rather, they are committed to using the knowledge and expertise they have derived from previous situations to help client organizations to function more effectively and efficiently. Management consulting requires a unique combination of specialized training, practical experience, and a high level of personal integrity.

Fourth is an emphasis on providing advice to the client in the area of dealing with *management problems* and issues. There are all sorts of consultants who deal with all sorts of services (personal image, product design, engineering, etc.), but these are not "management" consultants.

Fifth is the understanding that management consulting is a service which is usually provided *for a fee.* For the consultant to be truly objective, the recommendations must not be tainted by undue influences. Therefore, professional management consulting is not a "front-end give-away" promotion to entice a customer to buy a particular product or service arrangement. Management consulting is a conscious contractual agreement between two parties. The terms of the contract and the arrangement for the consultant to be compensated are usually spelled out in writing, although this is not required. For real consulting to take place, both the consultant and the client must mutually consent to legitimatize the activity; otherwise, it is little more than friendly advice.

As is obvious from the above, management consulting does not easily lend itself to a definition. It is not a product which fits neatly into a box that can be sold at a fixed price. It is an open-ended, almost fluid process where the changing needs of each client define and redefine this activity called management consulting. This being so, it is important to look at some of the reasons clients hire consultants.

WHY CONSULTANTS ARE HIRED

Consultants assist clients in many ways. For example, in the cover story of the July 25, 1994 issue of *Business Week*, new trends in the way consultants were being used were identified as follows:

1. Guidance in turbulent times as managers grapple with change, consultants are hired to help them identify ways for their companies to become more competitive.

2. To fight the fear brought about by change, consultants help overcome suspicion and skepticism by working side-by-side with managers to analyze operations, draft recommendations, and implement plans.

3. Stepping into the breach to fill management gaps created by downsizing, companies are turning to consultants for help on projects that once would have been done by staffers.

4. Ongoing assignments are becoming more commonplace as projects that no longer focus on a single area of the client's operations. Consultants are being engaged not just for months but for years to address the convergence of strategy, operations, organization, and technology issues.

To succeed in consulting, it is crucial to understand what clients are looking for from consultants. This seems obvious, yet far too many consultants fail to grasp its importance. Chapter 8 of this book is on Client-Savvy Consulting and deals more specifically with the issues involved. At the most basic level, managers will not hire consultants unless the consultant can provide something that is missing in the client organization. These needs will vary over time, and successful consultants carefully monitor their past, present, and prospective clients to be aware of changes in the organization or among their clients' competitors which can presage the need for the consultant's services.

Among the reasons consultants have traditionally been hired are the following:

▲ To supply extensive experience on a temporary basis. Consultants can devote full-time efforts to solving major problems, such as developing corporate, organizational, or marketing policies which, in the day-to-day pressure of running their business, leaves little time for the client management to focus on both operational and strategic issues. Consultants can provide both experience and time to address critical problems.

▲ To provide specialized knowledge and/or technical skills. Many times problems or situations confronting a client organization are beyond the internal capabilities of the client staff. The consultant can contribute special expertise on an as-needed basis; thus the client avoids the cost of having to hire additional personnel, especially in those cases where the problem is transitory. The consultant will leave once the job is completed.

▲ To give an impartial viewpoint. Client personnel are often influenced by their personal involvement or existing corporate traditions or habits, and as a result, may be unable to see the true problem or its full scope and to propose alternative solutions.

▲ Because the consultant is not subject to client corporate politics, the consultant can be impartial and unbiased in situations where no one from within the organization would be.

▲ To reinforce management decisions. Occasionally consultants are asked to undertake assignments to justify a decision already made by client management. That is, the client may know exactly where he wants to go and what his decision will be, but wants to have a consultant's report to support his views. This use of a consultant may not be unreasonable, but consultants must be careful not to accept assignments in which their services are misused or their objectivity is impaired.

WHAT CLIENTS EXPECT FROM CONSULTANTS

From 1979 to 1996, I was in a position where I provided prospective clients with referrals to consulting firms. Based on that experience, I compiled the following list in the order of importance of the attributes clients look for when deciding which consultant to hire:

1. Industry knowledge (e.g. financial services, packaged goods). There was a time not too long ago when the main value offered by consultants was their broad range of knowledge and an ability to apply insights and experiences gleaned from working in a variety of industries to the issues faced by the present client. This was the golden age of the generalist consultants where the application of sound business practices was perceived as being more important than specific knowledge about the industry in which they were being applied. Today, clients are confronted with a legacy of downsizing, specialization, and increased use of technology. Consultants are sought who have an in-depth knowledge of the client's particular industry to help the client deal with increased competition within that industry. Additionally, in many companies early retirements or outplacements have

depleted the ranks of experienced staff members, leaving the client with gaps in what he needs to know about not only his industry, but, in many cases, his own firm. Highly experienced consultants are then often brought in to fill these voids.

2. Functional skills (e.g., strategic planning, compensation systems). After industry knowledge, the next most important consideration expressed by prospective clients seeking to hire consultants was the functional skills offered by the consultant. This is not surprising given the fact that many companies have eliminated staff positions that were previously responsible for performing many of the jobs which subsequently are being farmed out to consultants. In fact, it is becoming increasingly common for companies to turn over entire operations or departments to consulting firms. This practice, known as outsourcing (or in some cases, facilities management), has allowed firms such as EDS, which was founded by Ross Perot, to become in effect the data-processing department for many large, well-known companies. This trend of outsourcing non-core practices continues to expand, with consulting entities like Towers Perrin now taking on the role of employee benefits administration for major clients.

3. Relationship management skills (i.e., "chemistry" or "fit" between the client and the consultant). Consulting is a people business, and no client wants to be treated as a number or as a "meal ticket." Nor does a client want to have to guess who to contact at the consulting firm to get a. question answered or to arrange an appointment. Clients want to have one person to call on who has the authority to respond to their needs. It is also important to remember that, to a large extent, a client will define a project as being successful or not successful depending on how he/she "feels" the project went. And positive feelings are generated by a sense that each party wants to do what is good and beneficial for the other. Another component of this sense of relationship sought by prospective clients is that the culture of the consulting firm fit with the culture of the client organization.

4. Experience (clients don't want to provide "on the job training" sites for new consultants). Clients want their consultants to be highly seasoned and experienced. They are not greatly concerned that you need to compensate senior people more highly, and therefore, to make a profit you need to leverage your project team with fewer senior people than junior. Nor are they usually interested in your need to gain experience for those who need more.

5. Global delivery capabilities (clients practice in the worldwide marketplace, and they want their consultant to be able to go with them). Even smaller companies today sell or want to sell their products outside the United States. Some have even opened marketing offices or manufacturing facilities in other countries, while others are seeking joint ventures or strategic alliances with other companies in other places. They want their consultants to be able to help them in a seamless manner wherever the client goes.

Problem-Solver 1-3
OUTSOURCING

The Issue

What's all this fuss about outsourcing?

Let's Work This Through

Many management consulting gurus have been advising companies to "stick to their knitting," i.e., to focus on the core activities needed to produce the product the company is in business to produce. This admonition to focus has caused many companies to look for ways to "rid" themselves of what they see as ancillary activities to their main mission. But many of these activities are nonetheless crucial to keeping the company going. What to do? Turn these operations over to consultants to run.

How does it work? Well, while each situation is somewhat unique, there are some generalizations which may help you to understand why this area of consulting is growing:

1. The client decides to outsource a particular activity such as data processing or employee benefits administration.

2. A consulting firm with expertise in that functional area agrees to take over the handling of the needed service.

3. The employees (most, if not all) of the client that were working in the area to be outsourced become employees of the consulting firm and continue working on the client's behalf.

4. The client saves on payroll costs and is better able to focus resources on core activities.

5. The consulting firm is paid by the client and/or receives a percentage of the cost savings experienced by the client.

6. The consulting firm can likewise focus on doing what it does best.

OTHER THINGS CLIENTS LOOK FOR

There are lots of things, both objective and subjective, that go into the decision making process when it comes to clients selecting consultants. While those listed above are the most frequently mentioned criteria, there are others which have been mentioned frequently enough to warrant listing here. These include:

▲ Consultants to help implement their recommendations and not just provide advice or a report and then leave.

▲ Performance-based pricing so the consultant shares in the risks and rewards of the project.

▲ Consultants who really listen to them and understand their needs, rather than having "preconceived solutions in search of a problem."

▲ High quality personnel to be assigned to their project.

Problem-Solver 1-4
LOTS OF ROOM

The Issue

Is consulting limited to a few fields of endeavor or is the field fairly broad?

Let's Work This Through

Depending on how finely one wants to dice up the industry, there are anywhere from about a dozen to nearly 300 principal services offered by management consulting firms alone, not counting other types of consulting such as public relations, executive search, outplacement, etc.

ACME and the Institute of Management Consultants each offer a referral service to help clients identify consulting firms and individual practitioners with the expertise they are seeking. Each of these referral indexes list 278 different areas of consulting expertise. Again, because of the evolving nature of the business, these lists must be updated regularly as new services are added.

WHAT KINDS OF CONSULTANTS ARE THERE?

At its broadest, the management consultant, as a change agent, assumes one of a few basic roles:

Resource Consultant or Process Consultant. Resource consultants provide expert or technical advice, service and recommend a course of action based on the consultant's prior experience in dealing with similar problems, thereby transferring to the client organization knowledge and expertise. This approach requires a correct diagnosis of the problems and needs of the client, effective communication between the consultant and client, and the consultant's experience and ability to gather information, transfer knowledge, and have his recommendations implemented.

Process consultants, on the other hand, attempt to help the client organization solve its own problems by making it aware of the internal organizational processes and providing the client with techniques for accomplishing change. While the resource consultant is concerned with passing on knowledge and solving problems, the process consultant is concerned with passing on approaches and methods so that the client organization can understand and correct its own problems.

In today's world of consulting, these two roles are not mutually exclusive. Indeed, the successful consultant has learned to use both roles in the same assignment to both position himself in the client's mind as an expert who knows what he is talking about, and to help the client to understand and use a process for solving problems in the future.

Diagnostician or Implementer. Diagnosticians are analyzers. They want to probe the problem as articulated by the client to get below the symptoms so as to identify the causes of the situation and thereby recommend a solution or action. These types of consultants are often used by large companies that have in-house capabilities to implement the consultants' recommendations.

Implementation consultants seek to bring about lasting change in the client organization. They point with disdain at the dusty reports left behind by the diagnosticians. They help the client implement recommendations as critical components of the consulting process.

Customized Solutions or Off-The-Shelf Products. Consultants vary considerably in the way they provide services to their clients. Many prefer to develop a unique solution to the specific and particular needs of each client. On the other side are standardized products such as software programs, training programs, and generic strategic planning systems designed to provide cost-effective solutions to generic business problems.

There is a lot of name calling and finger wagging between these two approaches. The customizers decry the commercialization and "productization" of consulting of those who offer standard solutions that are fit by force to a variety of client situations. The off-the-shelf group counter that there is no need to spend exorbitant amounts of money to reinvent the wheel.

Internal Staff Consultants or External Consultants. It should come as no surprise that large companies tend to have more management issues and problems than do smaller companies. The need for on-going continuous advice has led many of the largest corporations to develop internal consulting operations utilizing members of their own staffs as "troubleshooters" rather than always bringing in more costly outside experts. These internal consultants are intimately familiar with the client organization and are aware of the "landmines" and hidden agendas that can derail outsiders.

External consultants on the other hand, typically offer greater objectivity and a broader range of experience than do staff consultants. They are freer to make broader and more risky recommendations than their internal counterparts who may not want to jeopardize their careers or performance evaluations. Outsiders are less constrained by chains of command and often have greater access to the client CEO than do staff members of the organization.

Large or Small Firm. As can be seen by the distribution of revenues, the largest firms account for the greatest share of the consulting market. Their projects are typically quite large in dollars and scope and are performed for big companies. They rely heavily on leveraging the time of their senior partners, with much of the actual work being done by lower level or new consultants. Historically, the big firms were better at analysis than implementation, but this is changing to some extent.

Small firms and sole practitioners can provide more personal service on smaller projects. Typically they can charge lower fees because they have lower overheads than larger firms. With smaller firms, the senior-level and experienced personnel will work on the project since the sellers are also the doers, which is not always the case with big firms.

Specialist or Generalist. Generalists tend to diagnose problems in terms of a breakdown of certain management fundamentals or basic business principles. They look for root causes rather than seeking solutions for symptoms and believe that, because of their business training and experience, they are able to tackle a broad range of problems, regardless of the industry in which the client operates.

Specialists, as the term would suggest, would respond that in our complex and rapidly changing world, problems have become so complicated or technical that only someone with specialized expertise is truly capable of solving them. They would argue that generalists tend to simply skim the surface, while the generalist will counter that the specialist may be solving the wrong problem.

Generalists tend to be more effective in working with top-level management on complex issues where a comprehensive diagnosis is called for before attempting to implement solutions. On the other hand, when the client is relatively clear about

Problem-Solver 1-5
TYPES OF ASSIGNMENTS

The Issue

What are the basic types of assignment consultants are used for?

Let's Work This Through

While there are many different names attached to the practices, the most common consulting projects are:

▲ A management audit (or study, or appraisal, or diagnostic, etc.) in which the consultant surveys the client organization's resources, policies, and patterns to identify or define strengths and weaknesses and key problems.

▲ Special studies or surveys such as feasibility studies, market research studies, surveys of consumer or customer attitudes, HR studies, etc., and the collection and analysis of data for planning purposes.

▲ Providing solutions to defined problems such as organization design, information system recommendations, new compensation and benefits plans, plant layout, and material work flow.

▲ Assisting in implementation including training programs, turnkey systems, identification and selection of personnel.

▲ Acting as an advisor or serving as a sounding board for new ideas.

the problem, and the problem is of a technical nature, then the specialist provides a better option. Problems arise when consultants try to go beyond their capabilities or strengths, or when the client fails to recognize the fact that consultants are not miracle workers who can be used interchangeably to solve every problem. Successful management consultants realize and appreciate the value of telling the client when it would be appropriate to bring in another type of consultant to assist in the project. The consultant who tries to do everything often winds up doing it badly, and then no one benefits.

SERVICE AREAS AND INDUSTRIES

Another way of talking about kinds of consultants is to look at the industries they serve or the functional expertise or service they provide. For example, some firms provide a wide variety of services to a particular industry (the financial services industry, for example) while others may tend to focus on a particular function or service (such as employee benefits) which they offer to all types of industries. Some of the more common general classifications used by ACME's referral system are the following.

SERVICE AREAS

General Management

Manufacturing

Human Resource Management

Marketing

Finance & Accounting

Materials Management

Information Technology

Research & Development

Administrative Services

Specialized Services

INDUSTRIES SERVED

Agriculture/Forestry/Fishing/Mining

Energy/Utilities

Construction

Manufacturing

Wholesale Trade

Retail Trade

Finance

Insurance

Real Estate

Services

Communications

Government

Healthcare

High Tech/Electronics

Biotech/Genetic Engineering

FORECASTS BY SERVICE AREA

Information Technology (IT) consulting accounts for some 45% of the total consulting market and is expected to grow at about 10% per year for the foreseeable future. IT consulting includes such things as: client/server and workstation/PC applications, multi-media systems, networking, and Business Process Reengineering (BPR), which typically requires significant system changes. IT-related consulting is carried out mainly by the Big 6 accounting firms.

Human Resources (HR) consulting represents about 24% of the consulting market. The largest component of HR consulting is actuarial and benefits consulting where growth has been basically flat for the past few years. This is due in large part to relatively little governmental action in the form of new laws or regulations mandating new HR-oriented programs or services. Because of the maturation of the traditional marketplace, growth will come from such areas as outsourcing of benefits administration from corporations to consulting firms; healthcare consulting; risk management; and, with the restructuring of business, HR planning and development and organizational projects provide some bright spots.

Operations consulting is at the practical, implementation end of the spectrum and accounts for about 12% of the market. Production management, Total Quality Management (TQM), change management, and similar activities will help this area to grow at some 15% per year.

Strategy consulting firms that are able to help clients to implement their plans will do quite well, but on the whole, the traditional strategic planning consulting field will grow only moderately.

Financial consulting will grow only slightly, with areas of promise in the areas of international currency, interest rate swaps, and activity-based costing.

FORECASTS BY INDUSTRY

Financial Services such as banks and insurance companies are facing increasing competition and are turning to consultants for help. The reduction or elimination of boundaries between commercial and investment banks and insurance companies, coupled with competition from entities such as credit card companies (retailers, automotive companies, etc.), will help consulting services in this sector to grow by 10%–15% per year.

Retailing and distribution are undergoing change which always represents prospects for growth for consultants. The application of information technology, logistics optimization, and improving customer service while lowering costs are all areas of opportunity.

Telecommunications (or multi-media industries) such as telephone companies and cable, wireless, television, and cellular communications are converging, and growth in these areas is so explosive that consulting revenues should increase by more than 20% per year.

Public sector/governmental institutions are faced with the need to cut costs while improving service delivery. Consultants should find opportunities to help "re-invent" government and to transfer federal programs to the states. We can also expect continued initiatives in the *health care* legislation arena, and consultants will be asked by providers, employers, and insurance companies to control costs, improve quality, and ease public access.

Manufacturing activities in the U.S. have rebounded over the past couple of years, and reengineering programs are still going on. The way is being paved for consultants to help manufacturing companies accept transformational change and even to reinvent themselves to focus on strategic, mission-critical areas of their primary business.

Problem-Solver 1-6
NEW TRENDS IN CONSULTING

The Issue

So what's new in consulting?

Let's Work This Through

After interviewing consulting firms and client organizations, there appear to be several new trends emerging which bear watching. These include:

▲ A resurgence of contingency fee arrangements.

▲ Consulting firms are establishing contractual relationships with university professors to keep them in touch with cutting edge research and to serve as adjunct members of the consulting firm's staff as appropriate.

Continued

▲ From Andersen Consulting virtually functioning as a company's data processing department, to Towers Perrin handling human resources administration, consulting firms are providing outsourcing services to clients.

▲ Clients are operating globally, and they want consultants who can serve their needs seamlessly on a global basis, not merely internationally.

▲ More than ever, consultants and clients are working together as teams to solve problems.

▲ Clients are asking for more than reports from consultants; they want implementation and demonstrable results.

▲ The size and scope of many projects are becoming so large that few firms are capable of handling them.

So what lies ahead for consulting firms? What will take the place of today's business process reengineering projects that have provided much of the growth in consulting over the past few years? Well, according to an April, 1996 survey conducted by the Foundations for Excellence in Consulting and Management[6], an affiliate of ACME, client organizations over the next five years are going to focus on growth strategies rather than on cutting costs. The survey also found that consultants, clients, and academics agree that business strategy is the most important issue for future focus. However, clients tend to see marketing/sales issues as their next most important area for improvements, while consultants say information technology and academics point to human resources concerns as being "highly important."

We can be sure of one thing—that whatever issues, problems, or opportunities clients may face in the future, management consultants will be there to help them.

WORKPLACE TRENDS THAT WILL IMPACT CONSULTING

Perhaps more than most workers, consultants must pay attention to trends and changes that impact the business world as a whole. Six of these trends that may reshape the workplace dramatically are:

1. Smaller companies—The corporate behemoths of yesteryear appear to be going the way of the dinosaur. Massive workforces used to be a sign of strength and stability. Today, leaner is thought to be better, and payroll trimming often results in higher stock prices. Even companies such as IBM, which not so long ago epitomized lifetime employment, has cut its

workforce by nearly 100,000 people since 1985. In fact, the "typical" large firm reduced the number of employees by 20% in the last ten years. Many of these outplaced employees will seek to join the ranks of consulting. Many others will start up new companies and become clients of consultants. So, too, will the companies that have cut their workforces turn to consultants to fill many of the roles that they had previously relied on their own employees for.

2. New organizational forms—The hierarchical structure that was so familiar to most of us throughout our careers will be modified to deal with a new workforce that will demand more flexibility and more accountability. They will want to be evaluated and remunerated based on their knowledge and contributions rather than being tied to a position or a box on a meaningless chart. Traditional organizational charts are also being torn asunder by the elimination of entire functions and departments through outsourcing. Consulting firms like EDS and Andersen Consulting not only provide data processing services to their clients, but will literally become the data processing department of major corporations right down to hiring the workers who had previously run the department.

3. Technicians replace white-collar workers as the elite of the workforce—As the world becomes more and more automated, there will be more and more mechanical breakdowns. White collar workers who get dirty, technicians now represent some 15% of the workforce, and by the year 2000 are expected to climb to 20% or 23 million people, thus far exceeding the number of manufacturing and labor jobs.

4. Horizontal rather than vertical division of labor—Workers will be more devoted to their specialty or the work they do than to the company they do the work for. If working for a particular employer does not suit them, they will pack up their skills and move on. One might think of tomorrow's workers as analogous to a football team. Negotiations and deals rather than directives and mandates will be needed to motivate them, and bosses will be replaced by coaches and coordinators.

5. Service-providing, not product-producing, companies will predominate— Service businesses already account for nearly 75% of U.S. employment, and the numbers are expected to grow. Personal services that are designed to help reduce stress, such as mail and janitorial services, massage therapists, and certain health care professionals are the fastest growing fields of employment.

6. The meaning of work itself will be redefined—The technology revolution has made the 9-to-5 workday irrelevant as people work out of remote locations at times that are convenient for them. Lifelong learning to stay on top of change will dramatically increase the number of adult education offerings, and people will seek new ways of defining themselves rather than finding their identities in the work they do.

As these and other trends unfold, their impact on consultants will be powerful. For consultants who can take advantage of the forthcoming changes, it will be a time of excitement and profitability. New services and products will have to be developed to meet the needs of a very different clientele. More people with varied skills will be sought by consulting firms, but many of these new entrants will opt not to trade one corporation for another in the form of a large consulting firm, and will therefore set up their own practices. Consulting is indeed a growing business. But is it the right business for you?

The next chapter may help you find an answer to this question.

2
BECOMING A CONSULTANT

THE AGE OF DISCONTENT

As technology continues to dramatically change our lives and the way work is done, knowledge truly is power. In this world of lightning-fast change, the jobs of millions of workers are being altered dramatically. Technology and automation will cause factory jobs to dwindle as service positions grow. For many people, the jobs that once seemed so secure no longer are.

Those who will avoid becoming one of the unemployment statistics will be those who take control of their own careers. They will think of themselves as products to be marketed. The implications are significant:

▲ The definition of success is changing as people are not prepared to sacrifice their personal and family lives for the sake of their careers.

▲ Workers will feel less loyalty to their employers as they become more dissatisfied with impersonal work environments and authoritarian managers. Organizations will have to earn the trust of the people who work for them.

▲ Changing jobs is becoming the norm rather than seeking or expecting lifetime employment because people are looking for personal and professional growth.

▲ Self-employment and part-time temporary work is becoming an option of choice for many people.

▲ Outsourcing, alliances, and partnerships have changed the way organizations themselves relate to one another.

▲ Workers tend to see themselves as filling a role rather than having a job. The idea of being at a certain level is becoming less significant for pay considerations than performance and contributions. Expanding the abilities and growth potential of a worker's current position is becoming more important than climbing a corporate ladder.

▲ Technology is reducing the need for workers to be present at a central location during traditional "work hours" as people are able to work from home and even to relocate to places where they really want to live.

▲ In large corporations, outsourcing of non-core activities are allowing them to replace branches and divisions with integrated project teams.

▲ Companies are increasingly using contract workers to accomplish tasks on an as-needed basis. Many professionals will, therefore, be able to work for more than one company on more than one project when they choose to work.

▲ More companies are looking for professionals who have a variety of experiences and skills and can adapt to various job requirements.

Successful people in this era of sweeping change will be those who keep their options open. For many individuals, this desire for flexibility will lead them to consider careers in consulting.

SO YOU WANT TO BE A CONSULTANT?

There are several books on the market that provide in-depth, step-by-step processes to help you get started as a consultant. This *Insider's Guide* highlights some of the more valuable aspects of these other publications, and this chapter concludes with some self-assessment tools that I developed for use with people seeking career advice which you may find helpful.

Perhaps you've been thinking about it for quite a while now, or maybe it's a new idea brought on by the sudden awareness that your "safe" corporate job really isn't so safe. Maybe you're fed up with corporate politics, or maybe you just want to try something different. Whatever the reason, you've decided you want to become a consultant. Now what do you do?

GOING OFF ON YOUR OWN

First of all, you have to decide how you are going to practice, by yourself or as part of a consulting firm. As a sole practitioner, you will have the most freedom, but you will also bear the most risk. You have no one to report to (other than your clients), but you likewise have no one to share the costs of operations with. Telephones, marketing materials, secretarial assistance, and even business cards and letterhead all cost money, and the bills are all yours to pay. As in all of life, there are tradeoffs to be made. How

Problem-Solver 2-1
TAKING RISKS

The Issue

I want to make a career change, but I'm afraid to. What do I do?

Let's Work This Through

There is a series of stages most successful people go through in deciding to make changes in their lives. You can go through some stages more than once, but, in general, you are better off going through each stage rather than trying to bypass one.

1. Become aware that something is wrong (you feel lousy, you never laugh anymore, etc.).

2. Define what the real problem is and decide that a change is necessary.

3. It's normal to feel anxious or apprehensive about making a change.

4. Prepare for risk by gathering information, exploring various options, developing support networks, managing your money, etc.

5. Prioritize your options—objectively and intuitively.

6. Take action, commit to a goal, and follow through.

much is a sense of independence worth to you? And costs of operations are not the only consideration.

Establishing your own consulting practice means that you are responsible for bringing in all the business. Maybe you are one of the lucky few who can leave your present employer and bring some business with you. If you have been with a consulting firm up to this point and have decided to strike off on your own, you may feel that you already have some clients you can bring with you. Be careful, though; your previous employer may feel that those clients belong to the firm and not to you. Legal battles are often the result of such disagreements. Make sure you and your former firm have a clear understanding of what you can and can't do in terms of practice areas and clients.

More likely, however, you have not worked as a consultant before. You have no clients to bring with you, only a list of contacts and some good leads. You will soon learn that consulting as a sole practitioner can be very lonely. You have no one to bounce ideas off of or to provide technical competence in areas where you may be weak. Financial security will become a fond memory and a future goal because, as a solo consultant, when you are marketing you are not generating revenues, and when you are busy on assignments you will be hard-pressed to find time for marketing. Revenue streams tend to look more like roller coaster rides, while expenses continue to rise.

Problem-Solver 2-2
PERSONAL CHARACTERISTICS OF CONSULTANTS

The Issue

What does it take to succeed in consulting?

Let's Work This Through

In addition to industry and/or functional expertise, there are certain personal characteristics and attributes which are shared by successful consultants. These include:

▲ Good physical health and mental stability.

▲ Self-confidence.

▲ Drive and self-motivation.

▲ Integrity and ability to engender trust.

▲ Independence of thought coupled with awareness of personal limitations.

▲ Intellectual acumen.

▲ Objectivity and good judgment.

▲ Analytical and problem-solving ability.

▲ Creativity and imagination.

▲ Strong interpersonal skills.

▲ Ability to communicate and persuade.

I can assure you from personal experience that there is also a tendency for many new sole practitioner consultants to feel that they are "retired" or on vacation once they leave the familiar confines of the corporate workplace. Motivating yourself can be a real challenge when you are no longer punching a clock and your workday has no pre-set hours.

So how do you go about motivating yourself without becoming a victim of burnout? Well, for one thing, all of the successful solo consultants that I know have learned to use stress as a constant source of energy that enables them to get things done and to feel good about what they accomplish. Perceived as an energizer, stress can be a great motivator.

Other techniques recommended by psychologists include:

▲ Looking for and finding something that stimulates and/or challenges you each day.

▲ Talking to yourself in positive phrases, braging about yourself to yourself, respecting yourself.

▲ Being positive in your outlook, looking for the good in every person and situation.

▲ Keeping your sense of humor. Laughing at yourself once in a while.

▲ Keeping problems in perspective. Seeing mistakes as learning opportunities. Not making mountains out of molehills.

▲ Scheduling time for leisure activities, social activities, vacations, and rest, in addition to time for work.

▲ Protecting your health. Eating right, exercising, getting sufficient rest.

▲ Developing support systems and associating with people who motivate you in a positive way.

▲ Listening to your inner self. You often really do know what's right for you.

Operating as a solo consultant can be exhilarating and rewarding, but it can also be stressful and costly. Many sole practitioners try this way of operating for a year or so, decide enough is enough, and they re-enter the corporate world or join a large, established consulting firm.

FORMING A PARTNERSHIP

As an alternative to going off on your own or hooking up with a big firm, you may want to consider forming a partnership. Try to find someone whose technical skills complement yours rather than duplicate them, so together you can meet a wider range of client needs. Your partner should have goals and financial objectives which are similar to your own.

A partnership provides you with a sounding board for your ideas and allows you to market a wider range of services to an expanded list of contacts. You also have someone to share overhead costs and can level out some of the valleys in the earnings curve, since one of you can be marketing while the other is busy on a client arrangement.

However, a partnership is not an automatic panacea, since you will now have to deal with such issues as: one partner bringing more revenues into the firm, the sharing of resources, whose work takes precedence, and the petty irritations that are inevitable in the interactions of any human beings. Choosing the right partner may not be easy, but having the right partner can significantly enhance your chances of success in consulting.

Larger is not always better. By focusing and harnessing the power of *delivery, technology* and *mindset,* many small companies in a variety of industries have successfully competed against much larger entities. The same is true for consulting firms.

By forming strong relationships with other solo consultants, partnerships, or firms, small consulting organizations can establish virtual global delivery mechanisms. One example of this is the *European Independents* (EI), a contractual arrangement among several leading independent consulting firms headquartered in different countries in Europe. Each member firm serves its own clients in the country where the firm is located. When an EI partner signs a contract to provide services to an international client operating in and needing consulting service in several countries, the other EI partners serve that client in their countries as though they were all part of one single consulting firm with client relationship management and billings handled by the firm which sold the project.

Technology is another force which allows smaller firms to appear and function as if they were much larger. Good graphics, quick response times, data retrieval, and transmission capabilities all enhance not only your firm's image, but also its capabilities and scope of services.

And size is to some extent a function of mindset. Many large consulting firms, such as EDS (with thousands of consultants around the world), try to break their consulting teams down into groups of 10 or so in order to give their clients a sense of "family" and of personal concern for the needs of the client. Likewise, if you think of yourself or your firm as small, you will act and stay small. I know of many solo practitioners and small partnerships who are providing very valuable high-level consulting services at the top levels of the world's largest companies.

JOINING A FIRM

If you prefer a more structured work environment and career path, you should consider joining one of the larger, established consulting firms.

As part of a firm, you can spend more of your time consulting, since such things as rent, accounting, payroll, sales taxes, administrative support, insurance, etc. are provided by the firm. The tradeoffs come in the form of rules and procedures, hierarchical structures and company politics—many of the same reasons you wanted to leave corporate life to begin with. A firm does provide, however, a greater degree of security and stability and a greater opportunity to work as part of a team on larger, more challenging projects than you will have as a sole practitioner or even in a partnership.

DO YOU HAVE WHAT IT TAKES?

Chapter 6 contains more detail about the skills and attributes sought by consulting firms in the people they hire. But skills and attributes tell only part of the story. I am firmly convinced that in consulting, as in all of life, attitude more than aptitude determines altitude. An overwhelming desire to succeed, coupled with a conviction that consulting is the right job for you, will enable you to be more successful than the technical wizard who doesn't want to be in the business.

Over the past few years, I have coached, counseled, and spoken to many hundreds of individuals who have wanted to change careers or become consultants. In each case I have them engage in a series of self-assessment exercises to help them get in touch with what it is that they really want to do. Some of the forms that I use to help people with that process are included at the end of this chapter. I encourage you to take the time to complete them.

In addition to a personal commitment to succeed, however, you do still need to have some industry and/or functional expertise that clients are willing to pay for. Again, taking inventory of your skills will help. Get out your resume and mentally review your prior jobs and experiences; then list your experiences and abilities by industry and function. My list would look something like this:

Industry	Job/Title	Responsibilities/Tasks
Furniture	Sales Manager	Marketing and sales
Industrial Products	Contracts Manager	Negotiate and manage contracts
Transportation	Foreman	Supervise workers, scheduling, operations management
Various	Seminar Leader	Coaching, teaching, facilitating of strategic plans
Non-Profit	President	International management, developing consensus, initiating change
Consulting	Senior Consultant	Strategic and market planning, mergers and acquisitions, growth strategies

Problem-Solver 2-3
THE IMPORTANCE OF LUCK

The Issue

Successful people all seem to be lucky in addition to any special skills they may have. How can I improve my luck?

Let's Work This Through

There are two different kinds of luck. One is purely random luck, like winning the lottery. The other type of luck is the kind of luck that highly successful people seem to create for themselves and which allows them to take advantage of every opportunity.

Here are some steps to help you create luck for yourself.

1. Take action to pursue your goals rather than sitting back waiting for luck to find you.

2. Luck comes to those who believe in themselves and their abilities. Success (and luck) is 85% attitude, 15% aptitude.

3. Be passionate about your goals so you can seize opportunities when they present themselves.

4. Be prepared *before* the opportunity comes along. Keep yourself mentally and physically in shape. Read about and pick the brains of people you consider to be successful.

5. Persist and refuse to quit, even when things get tough. Winners are lucky precisely because they don't quit.

6. Be willing to start small and work your way up. Luck often has to be earned.

7. Have a clear vision of what you want, not just a vague notion.

8. Be willing to adjust so you can take advantage of new opportunities and directions.

9. Take risks, but not foolish chances.

10. Preparation + Persistence + Opportunity = Luck

After completing your list, you can review it to see if there are particular industries or functional tasks for which you can portray yourself as a specialist. If you have had a wide range of experience, you might wish to offer your services as a generalist able to bring diverse perspectives and fresh thinking to client problems.

THE NAME GAME

You've completed the personal assessment forms at the end of this chapter and analyzed your skills, and you've decided to become a consultant. Now what? Well, if you want to join a firm, the information in Chapter 6 might help as you prepare a cover letter, distribute your resume, and call to set up interviews. If you are planning to go off on your own or as a partnership, however, now is the time to select a name for your firm. Because once you put a name to your idea and register the name with your state's Secretary of State, your concept becomes a business.

Many firms are named after their founder (A.T. Kearney, Inc., for example) or partners such as Towers, Perrin, Forster & Crosby. You can follow suit, or you may choose to select a name that in some way describes what your firm does or its expertise, as in Strategic Planning Associates.

THE LEGAL ASPECTS OF GETTING STARTED

You've settled on a name and started thinking about the services you will offer. Now it's time to get a lawyer to help you select the appropriate legal structure (C-Corp, S-Corp, LLC, LLP, etc.) and an accountant to set up your books. Remember, you are establishing a company. It may cost you some money up front to hire an attorney to guide your steps, but it is worth it to protect yourself and your personal assets.

Speaking of protection, you should also find an insurance agent to review your insurance needs in the areas of life, liability, worker's compensation, etc. And then, there is the decision as to where your office will be located.

A name, address and telephone number, a bank account, and tax identification number, and you're in business. Now all you need are some clients.

BUSINESS CARDS AND PROMOTIONAL BROCHURES

People have to know that you are in business and how to get in touch with you before they can hire you. Business cards are a must. Local print shops can help you design a card with a clear and professional look that can be maintained across all of your supporting materials (letterhead, envelopes, etc.).

Your marketing/promotional brochure must grab a reader's attention quickly—say in less than five seconds. Therefore, your brochure must be brief, clear, easily readable, and present your services in terms of the benefits clients can obtain by hiring you. Your brochure should cover such points as:

▲ What do you do and for whom?

▲ What specific services do you offer, to what industries?

▲ Who have you worked for or consulted to in the past?

▲ Who are you, and what is your background?

Your brochure, like your resume, will not get you a job. What they will do, hopefully, is make a prospective client/employer want to learn more about you and how you can help them. Remember, you will be hired, not because you're a nice person or have a beautiful smile, or even as a result of your fancy stationery, but because you offer solutions and benefits that a client needs. This is one of the most important tips you will receive, so it bears repeating: *SELL BENEFITS, NOT FEATURES.*

BEGINNING THE HUNT

You have business cards and marketing brochures. Now you need someone to send them to. Make a list of everyone you know or have met that is involved in any way (workers, executives, association members, etc.) in the industry in which you want to consult. A well-maintained list is a crucial component of a consulting career. Send each of the people on your list a letter to let them know about your new consulting practice, and then follow up with telephone calls to try to arrange a visit. In most cases, the person on your contact list may not be able to help you directly; that's okay. What you want from them is some information about, or better yet, an introduction to people who they know can help you. Make sure you send thank-you notes after each meeting and for each referral. Not only is it courteous, but you don't want to fall victim to the adage, "out of sight, out of mind." If you want people to think of you, you have to keep your name in front of them.

BAGGING A CLIENT

Sooner or later your persistence will pay off, and a prospective client is going to ask you to prepare a proposal. Before you start hyperventilating with excitement, it is necessary to take an objective look at some tough issues, such as:

▲ Based on what you know about the prospective client's firm, is this the type of client you want to have and will be comfortable working for? If the answer is no, you will be better off waiting for another opportunity.

▲ Who will you be competing against? Ask the client up front, since it makes no sense to spin your wheels preparing a proposal for an assignment you have no chance of winning.

▲ Why is the client interested in you, and what can you do to make it easier for the client to decide to award the job to you? Again, it pays to ask the client direct questions. You may get lucky and get an answer.

▲ What will the decision be based on? Is it a matter of cost/fees, the time frame in which the assignment must be completed, the size of the project, etc.? Again, make sure you can deliver what is needed, within the time frame for the fees the client can pay. If you have a bad feeling, walk away.

If you decide that you want to work for this prospective client and can do the job he/she has in mind, it is time to submit a proposal. While each proposal will be different, there are a number of points to be covered in every proposal. These include:

▲ *Background and understanding of the issues.* This is the opening statement in which you restate the problem or issues to be addressed.

▲ *Scope of the project.* In this section you tell the client what you propose to do to solve the problem by outlining the focus of the project and the nature of the final report.

▲ *Methodology or how you will accomplish the work.* You will want this section to be specific enough the let the client know you can handle the assignment, but at the same time, not so specific that the client can use your ideas to do the job without you.

▲ *Schedule and deliverables.* In this section you establish the dates when the interim and final reports are due. You should also identify what kinds of things will be developed during the course of the assignment (reports, seminars, etc.) and who will be the owner of the materials produced.

▲ *Fees and costs.* Set forth the amount the client can expect to pay in both fees and reimbursement for expenses. Let the client know your billing schedule.

▲ *Resources to be provided by the client.* Specify what you expect the client to provide on site to help you in conducting the assignment, such as office space, secretarial help, and access to files and information.

▲ *Benefits and results.* Help the client to think of consulting services as an investment in his company rather than as a cost by highlighting some of the benefits he stands to derive from the project. Be careful, however, not to make promises you might not be able to keep under the proposed schedule or fee structure.

The final phase in bagging a client is to write the contract. The contract does not need to be long and elaborate, but it should spell out the scope and conditions of the assignment so both you and the client are protected and future misunderstandings can be avoided.

It pays to put the scope and conditions of the assignment in writing, regardless of the size of the assignment. The contract should be succinct and complete and, hopefully, understandable to both you and the client.

Many large clients will have their own standard contract formats which you will be asked to use. In such cases, do yourself a favor before signing them; have them reviewed by your own attorney to make sure you are not putting yourself, your assets, or your firm in jeopardy by signing a badly drafted or even illegal document.

In general, a Letter of Agreement or contract should include such things as:

▲ Scope of the engagement, including any phases and estimated range of time for completing each phase.

▲ Schedule or time for completion of the project.

▲ Fee basis, including professional services and reimbursable expenses.

▲ Staffing of the project from both the consultant and the client.

▲ Budget.

▲ Invoicing and payment arrangements.

▲ Confidentiality agreements.

▲ Signatures and date signed by you and the client.

Once the contract is signed by both parties, you are officially a consultant.

SELF-ASSESSMENT WORKSHEETS

The following pages of this chapter contain some worksheets for you to complete which can help you assess your interests, skills, and experience. By comparing your responses with the list of skills and attributes sought by consulting firms when hiring new people, you will be able to see how you compare.

TAKING INVENTORY

If you want to accomplish your goals in life, you have to know the tools you have to work with. List below 10 talents and abilities you have. Write down everything that comes to mind. Don't be embarrassed. Be creative! To be a successful consultant, you will need to use all of your assets. Before you can use them, you need to know what they are.

1. _____
2. _____
3. _____
4. _____
5. _____
6. _____
7. _____
8. _____
9. _____
10. _____

Now take a look at some things about you that may need a little improvement. Are you disorganized? Do you procrastinate? List ten of these things, and as you write them down, make a promise to yourself to work on correcting them. Review your list each week and see if you are improving.

1. _____
2. _____
3. _____
4. _____
5. _____
6. _____
7. _____
8. _____
9. _____
10. _____

SCORE A GOAL

Becoming a consultant may be a major goal in your life, but it may be only one of several goals. It is important to know where these various goals rank compared to each other.

Go through the following list and rate each item as a number 1, 2, or 3 goal in your life, with 1 being top priority.

	Priority	Commitment
Find a job I enjoy	_____	_____
Strengthen my relationships	_____	_____
Become more physically fit	_____	_____
Quit smoking or drinking	_____	_____
Enjoy more leisure time	_____	_____
Get closer to my children	_____	_____
Get more education	_____	_____
Buy a nicer house	_____	_____
Move to a better place	_____	_____
Live a more meaningful life	_____	_____
Make more friends	_____	_____
Lead a more adventurous life	_____	_____
Feel better about myself	_____	_____
Find true love	_____	_____
Become more spiritual	_____	_____
Do more for others	_____	_____
Have a greater impact	_____	_____
Inspire others	_____	_____
Learn new skills	_____	_____

Now go back through the list, and number the items 1 through 3 in terms of your commitment to do something concrete to achieve each of the goals.

1 =   I promise to take some concrete steps toward achieving the goal.

2 =   This is a goal I really want, but I don't have time to work on it.

3 =   This would be nice to have.

Now, focus only on those marked 1 in both categories.

DEVELOP AN ACTION PLAN

It is up to **you** to determine where you want to go in life and how you are going to get there. It is your responsibility to plan the future you are going to have. For each of the goals in the previous exercise you rated as both 1 in priority and 1 in commitment, identify concrete action steps you can/will take toward achieving it during each time period. Prepare a similar plan for each goal and review your plan daily. Remember, a goal not acted upon is merely a wish.

Short-term Goals (1 month):

1. _____
_____

2. _____
_____

3. _____
_____

Mid-term Goals (6 to 12 months):

1. _____
_____

2. _____
_____

3. _____
_____

Long-term Goals (5 to 10 years):

1. _____
_____

2. _____
_____

3. _____
_____

RE-ENGINEERING YOURSELF

Part I

If you **want** more out of life, you've got to **be** more. What kind of person do you want to be? What will you have to do? What will you have to know to become that person?

You can look at this exercise in terms of your life in general, or in terms of the type of consulting you want to do.

Describe the type of person you want to become:

What kind of preparation do you need to do to become that person?

_____

_____

_____

What do you love to do? What makes you HAPPY?

_____

_____

_____

How could you make money or spend more time doing what makes you happy?

_____

_____

_____

*What can you do **today** to take yourself a little closer to doing what you want to do?*

_____

_____

_____

RE-ENGINEERING YOURSELF

Part II

What would you really like to do to earn a living, either as a consultant or in some other way? What would you really like to do with your life? Think **BIG**, and put your imagination to work.

If I had the courage, I would:	But this is what stops me:	This is what I can do to overcome the things that stop me:
1. _____	1. _____	1. _____
_____	_____	_____
_____	_____	_____
2. _____	2. _____	2. _____
_____	_____	_____
_____	_____	_____
3. _____	3. _____	3. _____
_____	_____	_____
_____	_____	_____
4. _____	4. _____	4. _____
_____	_____	_____
_____	_____	_____
5. _____	5. _____	5. _____
_____	_____	_____
_____	_____	_____

Review your answers and work on overcoming these things that are stopping you from living your life to the fullest. Ask yourself *"What is the worst thing that could happen if I overcame my fear and went ahead to pursue my dreams?"* Visualize yourself taking action and totally succeeding.

RE-ENGINEERING YOURSELF

Part III

Complete the following sentences:

If I had my life to live over, I would

_____

_____

_____

_____

If I had my wish, I would

_____

_____

_____

_____

My life would be more fulfilling if

_____

_____

_____

_____

One person I highly respect is

_____

I spend most of my time

_____

One goal I really want is

_____

I am happiest when

_____

One area I need to improve in my life is

_____

I am most proud of my ability to

_____

Three things I would like said about me if I died today are:

1._____

2._____

3._____

PROS AND CONS OF BECOMING A CONSULTANT

After interviewing and consulting with and to consultants for 20 years, I have found that there are some commonalities of both pros and cons expressed by those who have chosen consulting for their lives' work. The pros include:

▲ Freedom to set your own schedule.

▲ An opportunity to earn more money.

▲ A chance to start and grow your own business.

▲ Helping others to run their businesses better.

But there are also downsides, including:

▲ Running a consulting business requires a lot of administration which cuts into your consulting time.

▲ The consulting business can be very cyclical, often to the point of feast or famine, so it is difficult to budget.

▲ The word "consultant" has been sullied by unqualified, unethical people hanging out shingles and entering the field.

▲ Consultants can only make recommendations. Despite your best efforts and the fact that the answer or course of action would seem to be readily apparent, there are times when the client simply will not follow your advice.

For successful consultants, the pros far outweigh the cons, and the idea that the next assignment may arrive with the next mail or phone call provides stimulation, challenge and excitement far in excess of the pitfalls. Say what you will, if you do decide to become a consultant, you may get frustrated, hassled, and stretched, but you won't get bored.

3
BUILDING A CONSULTING BUSINESS

THE BUSINESS OF CONSULTING

A few years ago I had an opportunity to meet with Fred Gluck, who at the time was CEO of McKinsey & Company, one of the largest and best-known consulting firms. During the course of our meeting, I asked him for his perspective as to where he thought the consulting business was going. Fred became quite indignant and responded, "That's just the problem, management consulting isn't a business, it's a profession, and people are turning it into a business."

There was a time when I first entered the field of consulting some 20 years ago, that I shared Fred's view. At least it certainly seemed that there was more of a professional atmosphere to the way consulting firms treated one another, and in the way their services were marketed (in those days no one would ever admit that consulting services were sold!). The major consulting associations had, and enforced, codes of ethics which precluded most forms of advertising, prohibited firms from trying to take clients away from another firm, and even had restrictions regarding hiring consultants away from another firm. Management consulting was practiced by a fairly small community of firms, and there was a perception that, as long as the firms did not try to grow too large, there were enough clients to go around. There was no need to aggressively compete. All that was necessary was to keep the clients happy. In the words of Carl Sloane, a founder of the firm Temple, Barker & Sloane (now part of Mercer Consulting), "You do good work, we all benefit; you do bad work, we all suffer." But by the late 1970s, things began to change.

By the beginning of the 1980s, the larger (and especially the so-called Big 8) accounting firms already had significant consulting practices. Fueled by the explosion in information technology where larger and larger projects required more and more manpower, and coming from a background where competing for clients was more the norm, the consulting divisions (at that time called MAS - Management Advisory Services) of the accounting firms entered and radically changed the world of management consulting. This is not to say it made the practice better or worse, but it has made a radical difference in the way consulting firms go about their business. Far be it from me to disagree with Mr. Gluck, or to disparage the monumental success of McKinsey & Company, but in my experience, the most successful management consulting firms are those whose people act and work like professionals, but whose firm operates in a sound business-like manner. While the firm may not want to admit it, McKinsey & Company has mastered this balance.

DO YOU WANT TO HAVE A FIRM?

After you have been in business for a while and have been successful in generating a number of clients, you will arrive at a point where you will have to make a decision as to the type and size of firm to form. If making money is of prime importance, than remaining as a sole practitioner firm or forming a partnership with a couple of people is the way to go, at least for a while. High billing rates and long hours mean high income, but extensive travel coupled with these long hours and the continuous pressure of marketing and delivering projects takes a toll on your health and your professional life.

Problem-Solver 3-1
RUNNING A SMALL FIRM

The Issue

In a few words, what is it like to run a small firm?

Let's Work This Through

If you decide that you want to start and grow a consulting firm, you're likely to find that:

▲ Starting and growing a firm is a constant stream of anxiety, frustrations, and near-failures.

▲ These negatives are more than offset, however, by feelings of being fully alive, involved, and engaged.

▲ You are at the center of activity, with the opportunity to make a difference in peoples' lives.

▲ If it's right for you, there's nothing to compare with it.

Starting a consulting firm can be very expensive, however. Suddenly you are back in the role of manager. You have payrolls to meet, workers to motivate and supervise, and all the other little (and large) details that go into running a business such as:

▲ Financial management and fiscal controls

▲ Human resources and hiring

▲ Office management and administration

▲ Advertising and public relations

▲ Legal issues and reporting

▲ Planning and organizing

If you are not going to perform all of these tasks yourself, you have to make sure that someone else is responsible for taking care of them. It is a natural tendency for you to want to spend all of your time doing consulting. After all, that's what you get paid to do. But the long-term success of your firm relies on good administration and proper leveraging. Plan your work well and master the art of selling, and you will make money, but failure to run your business properly will take all the fun out of it.

SOME BASIC ADVICE

You're the key to growth and success in your consulting firm. To a large extent, it is your ego that is on the bottom line—don't let your ego get in the way of sound business decisions.

Based on my experience and observations, here are some tips which may help you and your firm to be more successful:

▲ First, listen to the advice of everyone you respect.

▲ After absorbing what they've said, rely on your own experience, intelligence, and intuition when making decisions.

▲ Hire the best and brightest people you can. Surround yourself with individuals who make things happen, both in your own employees and in your subcontractors and suppliers.

▲ Don't focus on short term profits to the exclusion of long term profitability.

▲ Don't overfocus on growth and simply abandon the products, services, and clients that brought you to this point.

▲ Don't get so caught up in internal administration and management issues that you ignore your market, your clients and your competitors.

▲ Don't overfocus externally and disregard the need for management of your firm.

▲ Delegate, delegate, delegate. Help others to grow.

▲ Use every failure as an opportunity to learn and to understand how to become more client-savvy.

▲ Accept the fact that your role will change as your firm grows, from entrepreneur, to boss, to mentor. You will be called upon to share more and interact with clients less.

You are being offered a unique opportunity to lead and to create—use these gifts wisely.

WHAT TYPES OF PROJECTS WILL YOUR FIRM LOOK FOR?

Regardless of the exact words you use, there are basically three components to the mission of every consulting firm: providing your clients with high quality service, satisfying the needs of your staff members for challenging work and personal and professional growth, and achieving long-term financial success to keep the firm going.

Successful consulting firms are able to balance these three realities of meeting the needs of the client, recruiting and retaining good people, and meeting the firm's economic goals. Many factors go into this balance, but the most important is that of leverage, or the margin of income over staff costs and the ratio of senior, junior, and mid-level staff members.

The type of projects your firm most frequently works on and the skills needed by your consultants should be the main determinant of the mix of junior, mid, and senior consultants on your firm's staff. If most of your assignments require creative and innovative approaches to solving new or unusual problems, your firm will probably rely primarily on senior level, highly skilled people who are also more highly paid. There is relatively little opportunity to achieve much leverage of top people with lower level, less expensive consultants.

When most of your projects are the type which require more experience than innovation, you will want to hire people with a lot of knowledge about the particular problem or industry. Since you tend to know the issues involved, you can plan the project in advance and may be able to use junior people to do some of the work.

If your firm's forte is to address common or frequently recurring problems more effectively, efficiently, or objectively than the client's own staff can handle them, you may be able to use a higher proportion of junior people.

Your firm is likely to have projects of each type and several formats in between. How you balance the different types of assignments your firm takes, or a specialization in one area, will greatly affect your firm's hiring practices, financial strength, and organizational structure. Failure to align the types of projects with the right staff can have serious consequences for your firm. Having a highly experienced staff working on routine assignments will result in a bored, dissatisfied workforce billed out to clients at a

Problem-Solver 3-2
JUMPSTARTING GROWTH

The Issue

What can I do to build my consulting practice?

Let's Work This Through

While there are all sorts of things you can do, here are ten of the most common initiatives undertaken by consulting firms:

1. Determine who you want as clients. Learn the names and titles of the decision makers. Regularly send them useful information so they come to recognize your name.

2. Do outstanding work for your clients so they will not only give you references, but will proactively refer you.

3. Prepare case studies of successful projects to serve as the basis for articles and to supplement your marketing materials.

4. Make yourself visible by using every possible tool including articles, interviews, seminars, etc.

5. Write and distribute a newsletter.

6. Develop and use networks.

7. Make it easy for prospects and clients to do business with you. Be the one they want to work with.

8. Differentiate your firm. Put together a list of reasons clients should hire you.

9. If you can afford it, use advertising to reach large groups of potential clients.

10. Allocate resources, money, and time for marketing activities and programs.

lower rate than their salaries would demand. Problems that are too complex for a staff of relatively inexperienced or junior consultants is a sure-fire formula for client dissatisfaction. Successful firms carefully monitor their client mix, project mix, and staff mix to make sure they all support one another.

WHO WILL DO THE WORK?

In any consulting entity from sole practitioner to mega-firm, there are three main activities which are vital to successful operations: getting business, handling projects, and administering the firm.

As a sole practitioner, you wear all three hats. If you don't bring in the work, there is no work to be done. After you line up the client, you work on the project yourself, and/or oversee the activities of any subcontractors that might be used. You are also the person to whom the IRS and other regulatory agencies will look for the proper filing of all required documents, and on whose shoulders rests the mantle of management of business operations.

As firms grow, there tends to be more and more separation of these responsibilities. Senior level partners tend to spend a greater percentage of their time on marketing-related activities than on hands-on provision of actual consulting services. Very senior people are also likely to have firm and management responsibilities, while mid-level staff members are assigned to oversee the projects on which junior consultants work.

Often referred to as "finders" (senior level marketers), "minders" (project management), and "grinders" (junior level workers), the mix that the firm requires of each level is determined by the type of work the firm does, which in turn, impacts career paths within the firm. In some firms people may want to advance, but there may be no room at the next level, so people become dissatisfied and leave. At other firms, there are more or less formalized "up or out" policies where failure to advance means termination of employment. Either case provides an incentive to junior staff members to work hard and to continuously hone their skills if they want to succeed.

Problem-Solver 3-3
GETTING PEOPLE TO CHANGE

The Issue

I have a vision of where I want to take my firm for the future. How do I go about getting my people to go along with the change?

Let's Work This Through

It has been said that the only person who likes change is a wet baby. Change is not easy, so you will have to expect some resistance. To move ahead there are some things you can do, such as:

▲ Identify the sources of resistance and approach them separately.

▲ Involve the person(s) with the most resistance in planning the change.

▲ Be a politician and use persuasion where you can.

▲ Ask for ideas and suggestions from those who will be affected by the change.

▲ Don't wait for consensus. All you need is critical mass buy-in.

▲ When you have critical mass, commit to the decision.

▲ Communicate changes in person and follow up with a memo.

▲ Sell your decision and cover all bases.

▲ Set up channels for communication and feedback.

▲ Expect and manage fear.

▲ Remember, you're not going to get everyone on board. Some people will have to be dragged into the future kicking and screaming.

LEVERAGE—THE KEY TO PROFITABILITY

The ratio of junior to senior consultants is vital to providing clients with the proper service to meet their needs in accordance with the project for which your firm has been employed. And the proportion of lower- to senior-level people on your staff will, to a large extent, determine the level of job satisfaction among your employees. Likewise, the ability to leverage your top professionals is at the core of the success of your consulting firm.

To a large extent, your firm's profitability is tied to your ability to hire staff at a certain salary, and then to bill them out at multiples of that amount. For example, according to the 1996 ACME Survey of U.S. Key Management Information, consulting firms typically have a billing rate to earnings multiplier of 4.9 times. This means that in a typical firm, if an employee earns $50 per hour, then a 4.9 times earnings multiplier would translate to a billing rate of $245 per hour.

Looking at it another way, the typical hourly billing rate for employees earning the following amounts would be:

Annual Earnings	Hourly Billing Rates
$125,000	$238
$75,000	$175
$60,000	$150
$35,000	$87

By leveraging high-cost senior people with low-cost juniors, you can lower your firm's effective hourly rate, thereby reducing the cost to your clients while generating additional profits for your firm. With this in mind, you will want to carefully control the makeup of your project teams to ensure cost-effective delivery of services needed.

THREE PATHS TO HIGHER PROFITS

For many years ACME has published in-depth information about the economic and organizational dynamics of the management consulting industry. One of the major components of this data consists of the "Profit Model for Consulting Firms." Based on the "strategic profit model" originated by DuPont, the concept was adapted for ACME by Dr. David Maister, a well-known consultant to professional service firms, to analyze the return on investment for service businesses such as consulting firms. The "Profit Model for Consulting Firms" is based on the ratio of profits (before taxes or bonuses) per partner, which is the best overall measure of profitability for a consulting firm. Essentially it is a method of summarizing and viewing the interactions of margin management, personnel productivity, and staff leverage. As exemplified in the accompanying diagram, the measure of a consulting firm's profitability is determined by these three components.

Margin is defined as net profits (before taxes or bonus) divided by consulting fees. In order to achieve an acceptable margin, your firm must charge and collect adequate fees while keeping expenses under control.

Productivity is represented as consulting fees divided by the number of consultants, or consulting fees per consultant. Since consultants are the assets of a consulting firm (their time is what is being sold), "consulting fees per consultant" is similar to "asset turnover" in a retail, wholesale, or manufacturing business.

Leverage is the total consulting staff per partner, or the degree to which staff members other than partners are being utilized.

Multiplied together, the three components (margin, productivity, leverage) yield "profits (before taxes or bonuses) per partner". Increases in any one of the components (e.g., raising your fees while keeping costs in line, having your consultants work and bill more hours, or using fewer higher-priced people to supervise lower-cost juniors) will increase the overall profitability of the firm. Unfortunately, the reverse is also true. The interrelationship among these three components is easy to overlook because one can have a high margin, but only a mediocre productivity and/or leverage and still achieve an acceptable profit per partner. Highly successful firms, however, are aware of this interconnectedness and monitor overall profitability rather than just margin or productivity.

The "Expanded Profit Model for Consulting Firms" is reprinted with the permission of ACME and can be used to help you get a handle on how your firm is doing by filling in the information on your firm in the spaces provided. You can then compare your numbers to the results of ACME's survey of consulting firms conducted in the Spring of 19961 which can be found on the page following the Expanded Profit Model.

Remember, only increasing fees, lowering delivery costs, or better leveraging of your people will lead to better profitability for your firm, and consequently, to long-term success.

Expanded Profit Model for Consulting Firms Average

Number of Hours Billed**	x	Average Billing Rate Per Hour	=	Consulting Fees
_____				_____

Consulting Fees	+	Reimbursed Expenses	x	Total= Profits Expenses
_____		_____		_____

Profits*	+	Consulting Fees*	=	Profits/ Consulting Fees
_____		_____		_____

Consulting Fees	+	Total # of Consultants	=	Productivity
_____		_____		_____

Profits*	×	Productivity	=	Profits Per Consultant
————		————		————

Profits per Consultant	×	Total # of Consultants/ Total # of Partners (Staff Leverage)	=	Profits* Total/ # of Partners (Profits per Partner)
————		————		————

* Before taxes or bonuses

**Hours Billed refers to the actual number of hours billed to and collected from clients (or is the billable hours worked times the percentage of those hours that are actually billed and collected)

1995 PROFIT MODEL PERFORMANCE COMPARISON
(High versus Low Profit Firms)

High Profit Firms

Profits Fees		Fees per Consultant		Profits per Consultant
29.3%	x	$208,986	=	$61,233

Profits per Consultant		Consultants per Partner		Profits per Partner
$61,233	x	3.8x	=	$232,685

Low Profit Firms

Profits Fees		Fees per Consultant		Profits per Consultant
9.0%	x	$177,022	=	$15,932

Profits per Consultant		Consultants per Partner		Profits per Partner
$15,932	x	3.0x	=	$47,796

Mathematical relationships may not exactly total due to rounding.

All figures in the profit model are computed on a before-tax basis.

SOME KEY QUESTIONS

To succeed in consulting means paying attention, not only to your own business, but to that of your competitors and that of your clients as well. The following are some questions firms use to keep themselves on track.

1. Who is and who will be your competition?

    Conduct a realistic assessment of your competition on every project. Who are you being compared to by your clients? What other consulting firms are bidding for the same jobs you are going after? Today, more and more frequently your competitors may not even be firms, but rather sole practitioners. If you practice in a growing industry or service area, you can count on running into increased competition from both very large and very small firms. It is also worth bearing in mind the words of Roland Berger, founder and president of one of the largest European-headquartered consulting firms, Roland Berger & Partner, GmbH, who said, "My main competition comes not from other consulting firms, but from my clients." Remember, your clients have the option of trying to handle the problem in-house, of turning to one of their own outplaced workers and bringing them back in a consultant capacity, or of contracting with an outside consultant or firm.

2. Why should a client hire you?

    What makes you different from your competitors? It never ceases to amaze me how many consulting firm CEOs have told me, "We're going to be the next McKinsey," or in describing their firm's practices will say, "We're just like McKinsey (or Andersen, etc.) except we're smaller (less expensive, etc.)." To me that's the same as saying to a client, "Well, if you want the best, hire _____, but if you're willing to settle or don't have the money for the best, hire me." Instead, find a proactive way to differentiate yourself from the competition which highlights your own capabilities, experience, and expertise. Develop a list of "50 Reasons You Should Hire Us" in which you identify why clients should want to work with you.

3. What added-value benefits do you offer?

    When a client engages a consulting firm, they expect the consultant to be able to help them solve the problem for which they have been hired. Successful consulting firms are those which leave the client feeling that he got more than he paid for. On every assignment, look for ways to do slightly more than the contract expressly calls for.

4. How will you control the quality of the work?

   Even if you are a sole practitioner who handles every project individually, you are going to have to be concerned with the quality of your work product. The larger the firm and the more people assigned to the project, the greater the likelihood of problems with quality. Mechanisms must be implemented and enforced so that everyone in the firm understands and abides by the rules. Some common practices in place in different firms include: all proposals and contracts must be approved by legal counsel; all written materials going to prospects or clients must be proofread by someone other than the writer; a relationship manager is assigned to each client and is responsible for keeping that client happy.

5. Who will work on the project?

   It is easy to say that "the best person will be assigned to the project." But what if that best person is already busy on another assignment? How do you know who the best person for the job really is? And what if you have some staff members who are not busy ("on the beach," as it is called)? Can any of them be assigned to the new project? Questions such as these are driving more and more firms to implement mechanisms to better track the education and experiences of each of their staff consultants. In addition, as projects require ever more specialized expertise, even very large consulting firms are turning to the use of contract or per-diem help, often referred to as "stringers," "affiliates," "associates," etc. These highly skilled, highly experienced people often have their own specialty or niche consulting firms, in addition to their affiliations. The use of contract employees can reduce or eliminate the need for consulting firms to add staff members possessing infrequently called for specialties, but at the same time, increases the importance of quality-control initiatives.

6. How will you bill for your services?

   Traditionally, the most frequently quoted methods of billing by consulting firms are: fixed fees with expenses billed separately; time and expenses billed as incurred; fixed total price including time and expenses; and an annual or monthly retainer. Most firms ($\frac{2}{3}$ of those responding to a recent survey by ACME[2]) bill their clients monthly, and 80% of the firms surveyed bill expenses separately from fees with no markup. Another billing practice which is once again gaining popularity is that of so-called "contingency" billing. Under this scheme, a consultant is paid or receives additional revenues contingent upon the savings the client experiences as a result of cost-cutting recommendations made by the consultant or upon the successful implementation of a particular system. Contingency billing plans are popular with some clients who want the consultant to share in the risks as well as the rewards of their recommendations. They work best when the project is turnkey in nature, such as computer system installation. But in my experience, contingency or percentage of savings type of billing arrangements can place an unnecessary burden on the consultant's objectivity and independence, by possibly forcing the consultant to choose between recommendations which would mean higher short-term cost savings (and, therefore, higher fees), but which might not be in the longer-term best interests of the client organization.

7. How will your firm be managed, and by whom?

As consulting firms grow, they require more and more management. Yet most consultants I have met over the years have told me that one of the reasons they became consultants is that they did not enjoy being managers. In fact, almost every consulting firm CEO I have spoken with longed for "the good old days" when their time was spent consulting with clients rather than on firm administration. For this reason, some large consulting firms seem to have a "revolving door" at the highest levels of management where the top officers spend a fixed number of years (often 3-5) in their post, and then revolve back into a line position with direct client contact and responsibility. In the case of many mid-sized firms, there is often a president of the firm who is responsible primarily for the day-to-day management, while another person (often the founder-owner of the firm) functions mainly as a marketer/relationship builder and carries the title of chairman. For smaller firms, it is wise to outsource as many administrative functions as possible until it becomes necessary to add full-time staff functions.

8. How will you use non-billable time?

Billable hours refers to the actual number of hours spent working on client assignments and actually billed to clients. Even in the most successful of consulting firms, not all consultants spend all of their available time working on and billing for projects. A recent survey by ACME[3] found that between 20 and 32 billable hours were worked per week, depending significantly on the employee's position with the firm. Successful firms carefully track and make good use of those hours that are not billable to clients. Marketing and training are obviously important to spend time on, but what else do firms have their staffs doing? It is interesting to note the results of a recent ACME survey.[4]

DISTRIBUTION OF NON-BILLABLE TIME-U.S.
(% of Non-Billable Time Spent on Each Activity)
(All Reporting Firms)

	Senior Partners	Junior Partners	Senior Consul	Mgmt Consul	Entry Level Consul	Research Assoc
Marketing	42.3%	37.4%	27.6%	20.0%	11.6%	19.8%
Administration/ Financial Mgmt	25.9%	17.7%	12.5%	15.3%	16.8%	21.0%
Employee Recruiting	4.2%	4.7%	3.5%	2.9%	2.9%	2.7%
Personal Professional Development	4.3%	6.6%	9.3%	14.7%	24.2%	16.6%
Training Others	4.0%	7.4%	7.5%	7.1%	4.0%	1.8%
Non-Billable Travel	3.6%	3.2%	3.7%	3.4%	2.8%	1.0%
Vacation/ Holiday/ Sick Time	11.0%	14.9%	18.2%	20.9%	21.3%	15.9%
Other	4.7%	8.1%	17.8%	15.8%	16.4%	21.3%
Total	100.0%	100.0%	100.0%	100.0%	100.0%	100.0%

Source: ACME 1996 Survey of United States Key Management Information

TIPS FOR SUCCESS

The most successful consulting firms seem to have discovered certain keys that contribute to their success. Here are ten of them.

1. *The client comes first.* Make all decisions and recommendations with the best interest of the client in mind. This goes for everything from who you will assign to work on the project to the final report. If it does not redound to the long-term good of the client organization, it is the wrong decision.

2. *Profits aren't everything.* Too many consulting firms become so overly concerned about making profits that they harm themselves in the long run. Successful firms realize the importance of allocating money for technology, training, and new product and services development.

3. *Realize that mistakes happen.* In the words of the artist Salvadore Dali, "Don't worry about perfection; you'll never achieve it." Successful consulting firms consistently strive for high quality in their assignments, but they also realize that all human endeavors are marked by trial and error. Their consultants are encouraged to grow, which means allowing them to take chances and to learn from their mistakes.

4. *Be on the lookout for new opportunities.* Successful firms explore new ways to be of service to their clients, and they look for innovative techniques and products which can enhance their capabilities. Their consultants are trained to listen to their clients for indications of other problems the client might have and where the consulting firm may be able to help.

5. *Support free thinkers and those who challenge the status quo.* While all consulting firms devote considerable time and money to developing and fostering a certain image and indoctrinating their staff consultants in the firm's proprietary methodologies and techniques, successful consulting firms realize the importance of supporting and encouraging a few mavericks who challenge "the way things have always been done."

6. *Have a clear idea of what the firm stands for and where it is going.* Successful firms instill in their staffs a commonly shared belief in the mission of the firm. In addition, top management communicates a vision of what lies ahead for the firm. By doing so, everyone understands why the firm exists, what its priorities are, and shares a sense that they are contributing to helping the firm achieve its goals.

7. *Professional services firms are businesses.* While consulting firms exist to be of service to their clients, they are also companies or partnerships and must operate in accordance with sound business practices. This means promptly billing clients for services rendered, carefully controlling costs, sound fiscal management, adhering to responsible human resources policies, etc. These administrative details may not be as much fun or as exciting as solving client problems, but paying attention to them is crucial to success.

8. *Take time to look inward.* Consultants and consulting firms regularly scan their external environments and focus on issues of importance to their clients. This is as it should be. After all, consultants are often brought in

because of their broad knowledge and experience. But successful firms recognize that they also need to be introspective, so they stay in tune with their mission and vision. They regularly engage in management and even staff retreats using outside facilitators to help them look inward at their own operations. Likewise, successful firms recognize that consulting is a high-energy, stressful occupation, so they make sure their staff consultants and managers take their allotted vacation time and have an opportunity to focus on themselves and their families.

9. *Recognize that their staff is their most important asset.* While consulting firms may be justifiably proud of their technology, methodologies, products, and services, the most successful firms are organized around their people. Rather than simply putting people into boxes in a traditional organization chart, consulting firms often have much flatter structures with greater individual latitude and decision-making responsibility. It has often been said that "the true capital of a consulting firm goes up and down in the elevator every day." The quality and capabilities of their people is the true differentiation among consulting firms.

10. *Always look on the bright side.* Successful consultants are by nature optimistic. They have to be. After all, who wants to hire someone to help them solve a problem if the person they hire is a pessimist and doubts the problem can be solved? Remaining upbeat and positive helps the client to be optimistic as well, and therefore, more willing to accept the consultant's recommendations and better able to handle the stress of dealing with change.

WHAT DO YOU NEED TO COMPETE TODAY?

In the previous chapter I identified several new trends that are changing the way consulting is done today. Based again on my interviews with clients and consultants, here are some of the things consulting firms need to do if they are to respond to the increasing demands of clients:

▲ To develop and use a knowledge base of worldwide best practices.

▲ To have global teams of industry specialists, either members of the consulting firm's staff or through strategic alliances with other firms or sole practitioners.

▲ To provide a single point of contact for each client so the client has one person from the consulting firm to turn to with questions.

Problem-Solver 3-4
THE ROLE OF THE LEADER

The Issue

I hear a lot of talk about leadership today. What's wrong with just being the boss?

Let's Work This Through

When you run a consulting firm, you are dealing with highly intelligent, highly motivated professionals. While they may follow a leader, they will never cower to a boss. They will accept coaching, but resist bossing. Think about it, boss backwards is the same as a backwards boss—a Double SOB.

Your role as a leader in tomorrow's successful consulting firm will be to:

1. Be a servant leader with a sense of commitment to your staff and clients.

2. Create and communicate a vision for the firm.

3. Promote and initiate change to respond to ever-changing environments.

4. Build partnerships both internally among groups or lines of business within the firm so that they can support one another, and externally in the form of relationships and joint ventures.

5. Value and manage diversity in a world of hazy geography.

6. Manage information and technology to gather, analyze, and distribute information.

7. Achieve balance both in your own life and by helping your staff members achieve it in theirs.

▲ To offer customized solutions to the real problems of the client rather than "off-the-shelf" answers to preconceived issues.

▲ To have a technology infrastructure to support all these changes.

SOME NEW PROBLEMS FACING CONSULTING FIRMS

Again based on my experience as a consultant to consulting firms, the following issues are becoming very problemsome:

▲ How to pay for all of the new technology consulting firms need today.

▲ It is true that information is power, and the competitive nature of most consultants usually inhibits the sharing of power. So, while firms understand the need for improved "knowledge-ware" and data bases, it is difficult to make consultants share information by entering the data required for the systems to be effective.

▲ Globalization necessitates the integration of different cultures. But cultural differences can impede communications and lead to misunderstandings.

▲ With the size of some projects, particularly those involving the provision of outsourcing services which requires large numbers of people and a heavy infusion of cash, it makes me wonder how much longer partnerships like Andersen Consulting can continue to compete against publicly-traded corporations like EDS.

In addition to their "special" problems, consulting firms are impacted by the same problems that are affecting leadership decisions in all businesses today. Some of these major trends and their implications are:

Speed—People today want and expect instant gratification and response. As a manager of a consulting firm, you must constantly be on the lookout for bottlenecks which may be slowing down your response times. These impediments can be found everywhere from the number of times your firm's telephone rings before someone answers it, to signing off on proposals, to delivering the final report. Patience may be a virtue, but it is a virtue you will find sorely lacking in most of your clients.

Convenience—Not only do most people expect you to respond quickly, but they want you to fit into their schedule. If your client works on weekends or nights, he may quite well expect his consultant to likewise be available during those times. The need to accommodate client's schedules can often cause a conflict with your staff members who are seeking more time for themselves and their families and are not as willing to give up "their" time. You may often find yourself having to balance these competing forces.

Changing demographics—It has been estimated that by the year 2050, African-Americans, Hispanics, and Asians will represent one-half the population of the United States. An ability to speak more than one language and being comfortable with diversity are already practically requirements in most segments of the business world. Yet consulting firms have historically been by-and-large "old boy" clubs of white males. This is due in large part to the fact that until quite recently few women and minorities attended graduate schools of business. These schools are the "hunting grounds" at which consulting firms do most of their recruiting for new talent.

Lifestyle changes—Flex-time, elder care, child/teenage care, an emphasis on fitness and wellness with concurrent changes in eating habits, etc., coupled with a desire for more balance and personal time are changing the way consulting assignments have traditionally been staffed at many firms. This can be a real problem if your engagements call for the work to be done at the client location over an extended period or with a lot of travel involved. Many consulting firms have responded by establishing regional offices in proximity to large or numerous clients. Of course, doing so adds to overhead costs, administrative complexities, and a new set of staffing issues, such as the need for the ability of each office to provide the full range of your firm's services.

Choices—In a typical supermarket the largest amount of shelf space is taken up by sugar-coated cereals, followed by bottled waters. There are 1000 varieties of sneakers, 500 models and makes of automobiles, 138 kinds of toothpaste, practically innumerable beers and soft drinks, and more than a million different airfares for more than 500,000 daily flights! If you think the buying public is going to be satisfied with a plain vanilla, one-size-fits-all approach to consulting, you are in for a rude awakening. You will have to be flexible and enticing in the marketing and delivery of your services.

Discounting—While I have not yet seen billboards or commercials advertising "Special, one week only" sales on consulting projects, it is not beyond the realm of imagination in light of many of the discounting and other non-traditional fee arrangements I have seen recently. "Low-ball" and even free front-end services are being offered as firms try to get a foot in the door in the hope of landing add-on or downstream revenue-producing projects and relationships. More and more clients are asking consulting firms for contingency fee arrangements under which the consulting firm gets paid contingent upon achieving cost cuts or market increases of an agreed upon size. Personally, I am opposed to any arrangement that can jeopardize the consultant's objectivity, which I believe many of the practices can do. You will have to decide for yourself how your firm will respond to the expectations and demands of your clients.

Value-added—Consultants have instilled in the minds of the business public the notion of continuous improvement and upgrading. The notions of "if it ain't broke, break it," and "if it works, it's obsolete" are now being played back to consultants by clients who want to know "what have you done for me lately?" Value has become a given expectation, and simply delivering what you promised is not enough. When dealing with clients you must find ways to instill in them the notions that they are getting more than they paid for, and that the benefits they derive from your assignment will in some way positively affect their organization beyond the scope of the engagement.

Customer service—Clients are busy people, and they are demanding people. They have a right to expect good service, and you have an obligation to provide it. They should not have to contact a half dozen different people in your firm when they want to get an answer to a question. They want you to be flexible in your approach, but consistent in the quality of your work. Clients want to be kept informed of the progress of the project and to be asked for their input. Remember, clients aren't an inconvenience, they're the reason you're in business.

Technology—When used effectively, technology enables small firms to compete with large firms and, because of overhead differences, to win a considerable number of engagements. But the adage from the early days of the computer revolution – "Garbage in, garbage out"– still applies. The ability to gather data quickly can lead to too much data being collected, resulting in dataparalysis. Data and even information are wonderful – when they are translated into useful and useable knowledge. In fact, the need to manage knowledge is probably the main issue facing most consulting firms today. Technology is a major part of the knowledge-management puzzle, but technology is just a tool. People are still the key component.

Quality—Perception is the key to quality. The only true reality for a consulting firm is the attitudes of its clients. Successful firms take the time to regularly survey their clients at the completion of assignments to learn not only what went right, but equally, if not more important, is to learn what could have been done better. In many types of consulting engagements it is difficult to come up with an empirical measurement of quality, and even where objective criteria do exist, the subjective "feeling" that the project was successful is what the client is most likely to remember. To be successful in consulting, both the steak and the sizzle are important. And both must be of the highest quality.

EXPERTISE NEEDED BY LEADERS

Management skills are not enough to insure the success of your consulting firm. You have to be a leader. And leaders of tomorrow's firms will need to have a unique set of skills. A recent survey of more than 1,500 chief executive officers of cutting edge organizations identified a set of skills which they said will be required to lead companies in the 21st Century. The following four features were at the top of the list:

Problem-Solver 3-5
SHORTCUT TO SUCCESS

The Issue

In a nutshell, what can I do to give my firm the best chance of succeeding?

Let's Work This Through

Success must be earned through perseverance and hard work. There really are no shortcuts, but here are some tips as to what to focus on:

▲ Stay close to your clients' thinking.

▲ Track trends and their impact on your clients.

▲ Constantly improve your service and your services.

▲ Create a vision for your firm and strive to reach it.

1. Strategy formulation—An ability to create strategic plans and know precisely how and when to initiate them.

2. Human resource management—The effective handling of people is indispensable to sustaining top performance and achieving a competitive advantage.

3. Marketing and sales—Develop and demand an emphasis on client responsiveness and marketplace needs.

4. Negotiation/conflict resolution—The next century promises to be a time not only of rapid change, but of perpetual conflict brought about by such forces as hostile takeovers, litigation, and corporate espionage. In addition, there will be an increased emphasis on the need to balance multiple (often competing) stakeholders and more diverse groups of people.

WATCHING THE MONEY

The primary reason for the failure of consulting firms is not enough work/clients. The second most common reason is lack of financial control. Your firm must develop and use time and expense reports so you can prepare invoices and send them out at the end of each month. You must also monitor who has paid you, and most importantly, you need to have an accurate forecast of your cash flow so you can pay your people and your bills.

A cash flow forecast should be prepared monthly and should include a projection of actual billings and receipts from assignments your firm is working on, and a realistic estimate of new business you are likely to derive from new clients. Without a cash flow document, you won't know if you are likely to be able to meet your financial commitments.

Time and expense reports require each consultant to record daily the hours spent on particular assignments, as well as time used for other activities (marketing, training, administration, etc.). Filling out forms is not a favorite pastime of most consultants, but accurate time and expense reports are mandatory so you can bill clients appropriately.

The billing sheet is compiled from the time and expense reports and forms the basis for the invoice which is sent to each client. The client manager can also use the billing worksheets to compare fees and expenses billed versus budget.

Another form you will need is a personnel assignment report to identify and track work assigned to each consultant. This helps you to identify those who are working, those who are "on the beach," and those who are overloaded. This form is also useful to help you track the various experiences and types of projects each of your people has had over time.

PLANNING AND ORGANIZING YOUR FIRM

When you are operating on your own as a sole practitioner, you decide what business strategy to pursue, and the only work to be organized is that which you perform yourself or give to subcontractors.

As your firm grows, you will be faced with the challenge of planning your firm's continued growth and deciding how your firm needs to be organized. The organizational structure of your firm will vary based on the markets it practices in and the nature of the services it offers. Some firms are organized around geographic regions with offices in various cities to provide clients with the perception that they are dealing with a "local" firm. Other consulting firms are structured around industries with a partner in charge of financial services clients, and another partner responsible for clients in the utilities field, etc. For another group of firms, alignment around functional areas such as benefits and compensation or strategic planning work best. The key is to be aware of different organizational options and to develop profit centers around which your firm can be managed.

Making informed choices is the essence of planning. A plan gives your firm guidance and direction and keeps it from being torn in several often competing directions. Left to their own devices, each partner or practice leader in the firm will try to steer the firm in the direction of his or her own interests. A coherent and clearly articulated strategy keeps your firm aimed at its targeted market niches and avoids having it try to become all things to all people with the result that nothing is accomplished.

Your firm's strategic plan reflects decisions you have made with regard to such issues as: whether to grow or remain small, to offer a few select services in a particular market area, or to offer those services across industries, to be regional, national, or international in scope, and so on. These issues are interrelated, and a decision made in one area will impact your choices in the other areas. Therefore, your firm's strategic plan requires the participation of your key staff people in order to gain consensus for the plan.

It also bears remembering that your plan must be flexible and updated regularly at a planning retreat so that it will enable your firm to respond to a dynamic marketplace.

DEVELOPING A STRATEGIC PLAN FOR YOUR FIRM

Over the years I have helped dozens of consulting firms to develop and review their strategic plans. Many of these firms offered strategic planning consulting services themselves to their clients, but they understand the importance of using an outside facilitator to lead them through the process, unburdened by firm politics or a need to defend the past. I recommend a semi-annual or annual off-site retreat, away from the firm's offices and to which all key staff members are invited. It should encourage open and frank sharing of ideas and focus on new opportunities and plans for the future. As part of the preparation for the retreat, I ask the participants to respond to a series of questions. Among the questions are the following, which I consider to be key in developing a coherent thrust for the firm:

▲ *What business are we in?* It is amazing to see the variety of answers I usually get to this question from different staff members of the same firm. If your staff can't agree on what business your firm is in and know how to define it, how can you expect them to effectively engage in marketing activities for your firm?

▲ *Whom do we serve?* Here, too, there is often a wide diversity of responses. Each practice leader tends to respond from his or her own viewpoint as to the clients they target, which is understandable. Responding to this question helps your staff members to think in terms of the bigger picture of your firm's client base.

▲ *What services/benefits do we provide?* Again, it is often interesting to find out how parochial your staff may be, and how little they know about the breadth of the firm's practices.

▲ *What services/benefits should we provide?* Responses to this question can lead to a lot of food for thought and might suggest some real opportunities.

In addition to thinking about how you and your staff members might respond to the questions above, prior to embarking on the development of a strategic planning effort you should remember the Ten Golden Rules of strategic planning as identified by Ernst & Young, LLP, one of the Big 6 accounting firms.[5]

1. The doers must be the planners. Strategic planning should be undertaken by those responsible for the plan's implementation. Your firm's management must be involved, with an outsider serving as facilitator.

2. The "soft" issues (e.g., vision, beliefs, mission, and values) are more important than the "hard" ones (e.g., costs, headcounts, and growth projections). In a world of accelerating change and unprecedented competition, issues that were once considered "hard" are now "soft," (i.e. erratic, unreliable, and subject to unpredictable change). To create a foundation for planning and adjusting to change, you must find ways to make the "soft" issues "hard" (i.e, predictable, consistent, and stable).

3. Measurement is essential to recognizable achievement. Mission and goal statements are only practical if they have quantified objectives that define their accomplishment in any given time period. These objectives are unlikely to be reached unless they have equally specific strategies (i.e., resource commitments) focused on their achievement.

4. If the effort does not result in action plans, it is probably wasted. An action plan consists of a task, a time frame in which to accomplish it, and the responsibility for undertaking it.

5. Strategy development is more about choice than analysis. The determination of strategy is ultimately a choice in the face of uncertainty (i.e., the absence of perfect information).

6. Strategy implementation is more about commitment than correctness. When a plan has commitment, minor imperfections will be overcome by sheer momentum.

7. Change will occur, either by choice or design. Strategy is the deliberate attempt to beat evolution. In today's dynamic environment, the management of change is the central purpose of strategic planning.

8. Strategic change is about managing people, not money. If the day-to-day behavior of your people does not change, then neither will your firm's strategy.

9. Practice works; preaching does not. Your firm's people must be shown that there is no gap between words and actions. Only consistency of actions and statements, beginning at the highest organizational levels and consistently applied over a period of time, will result in fundamental change.

10. There is no one right dogma for anything. Every consulting firm has a strategy—some articulated, some not; some well-conceived, some not. The best of these strategies are formulated in written plans that can be communicated clearly and concisely. They are built upon a foundation of comprehensive basic analysis, sound strategic principles, and responsiveness to the patterns of change occurring around and within the firm.

4
MARKETING AND SELLING CONSULTING SERVICES

Your firm may hire the best people, use all the latest technology, have great methodologies, and go out of business if no one hires you. Even well-known firms like McKinsey do not sit back and wait for the phone to ring or clients to walk in the front door. They become well-known because of their marketing efforts, and they stay successful because of their ability to sell.

ELEMENTS OF MARKETING

Mention the word "marketing" to a group of consultants, and you will get a number of responses as to what the word means. Some may think we're talking about brochures or promotional pieces. Others will envision developing and maintaining personal relationships, while still others will talk about the importance of writing articles and giving speeches.

In fact, each of these ideas is correct, but they are individually only part of the answer. Successful firms operate on the realization that developing new business requires a cohesive approach along several different, yet complimentary and mutually supportive elements:

▲ Promotion—To get business, prospective clients have to know that you are in business. Promotional activities are designed to stimulate inquiries for more information about your services, to generate leads, and to pave the way for additional contacts between your firm and those who might hire you. Promotional techniques include such things as: speeches, seminars, newsletters, articles, public relations programs, and, recently, advertising. The objective of promotions is to broadcast your firm's message to (hopefully) a large audience.

▲ Networking—When done correctly, networking is the art of helping others to help you get more business. Networking entails a lot more than asking

---

Problem-Solver 4-1
ENHANCING CREATIVITY

The Issue

How can I become more creative?

Let's Work This Through

Creativity is essential in marketing. Creativity can be learned, and there are many techniques and courses offered for doing so. In general there are a few common threads and ideas, such as:

▲ Define problems in simple terms and break big problems down into bite-sized pieces.

▲ Ask questions—who, what, when, why, how, where.

▲ Allow time for reflection and thinking.

▲ Establish and meet with a "mastermind" group of people from within and outside the field of consulting and your area of specialization to share ideas and insights.

▲ Read extensively, including children's books.

▲ Look on the lighter side.

---

your friends to give or send you business. Effective networking begins with a desire to help other people. By helping others, you give them a reason to want to help you. The key is to give without expecting a "quid pro quo," because once you start "keeping score" of what other people are doing for you compared to what you have done for them, you begin to get selfish, and selfish people are notoriously poor networkers. Networking is based on a combination of gratitude and trust, and because networking takes time and effort, to be successful at networking requires motivation. You have to let other people know what you do and figure out who knows whom so appropriate introductions can be made. Networking is one of the strongest business development techniques for consultants and consulting firms, and has the effect of greatly expanding your sales force and bringing you business.

▲ Enticing or Courting—Promotion helps you reach groups of prospective clients, and networking gains you introductions. Now you have to focus on enticing or courting specific clients one at a time. Learn as much as you can about the target of your interest, both on an individual as well as a corporate level. Review trade association directories and Who's Who books for descriptions of key individuals, and annual reports, association publications, and 10-K forms for information about the companies you are interested in. You want to find out where this prospect's "hot buttons" are or what "turns them on" which, in turn, will help you to understand the purchasing process. It may help at this stage to put yourself in the client's shoes and think about how you would respond to your firm's marketing approach if you were a buyer. Ask yourself the same kind of questions your clients are asking, and analyze your answers to them—Why should I hire you? (What unique benefits or expertise does your firm offer to help the client solve his problem?) Would I want to work with this firm? (How responsive are we, how easy do we make it to do business with us, how friendly, conscientious, etc.) When a client hires a consulting firm, they are seeking to enter into a relationship with that firm. Therefore, your marketing process should be viewed as a courtship.

▲ Word of Mouth Marketing—You can talk all you want about yourself or your firm's capabilities, but when a client says wonderful things about you, other prospective clients are much more likely to listen. This means that a major component of your marketing efforts should be devoted to keeping your existing clients not just satisfied, but "delighted" with your work. The goal is to have your clients become your fans who proactively seek opportunities to recommend you to their colleagues at other companies who might have need of consulting advice. Word-of-mouth marketing has to be earned and requires effort on your part. The client expects you to be technically competent, so doing good, quality work will leave the client satisfied if your recommendations work. But to get your client to become "part of your marketing team" requires more than technical excellence. The client is not simply buying a product, he is buying peace of mind, trust, and reassurance. In effect, a client does not use a consultant, a client experiences a consultant. This means that your marketing efforts must be geared to a client's perceptions, as well as to his expectations. The client's true needs must be understood and met. Unfortunately, too many consulting firms overlook the importance of being "client-centered", and become enthralled with their own technical prowess or intellectual capabilities to the point where I have too often heard consultants lament, "This would be a great project if the client would get out of the way." An attitude like that is not lost on the client, and would certainly not lead to that client's becoming one of your raving fans.

▲ Caring and Nurturing—Not only do you want your present clients to be so happy with the work you have done for them that they are willing to tell others about you, you also want them to give you additional work themselves. Clients want to feel that their consultant cares for them and is not merely using them to beef up their client list. Nor do clients want to be taken for granted. Future business must be earned, yet many consulting firms that have well-structured programs for business development from new clients fail to have an organized plan for getting new business from present clients. This is ironic, since most consulting firms recognize that their best source of new business is from their existing client base. So why do most firms devote most of their time, effort, and marketing dollars toward new clients rather than on the care and nurturing of existing clients? One reason I often hear is that it is "more fun" to bring in a new client than it is to generate additional business from a present client. Then, too, firms tend to value and reward more highly those who bring in new clients versus those who may bring in the same level of billings in new business from present clients. If your firm wants to be fully successful, you will have to take advantage of the opportunities presented by your present clients.

▲ Market Research—If you really want to be effective in marketing, you have to know what is going on in the marketplace. The better you know what your clients and prospective clients are thinking and what they want, the more likely you will be able to convince them that you can meet their needs. If you want to know what your clients are thinking, ask them. But ask them in a systematic and organized way, and then listen and respond to what they have to say. Successful firms invest in market intelligence rather than basing their business development activities on guesses or assumptions. They also have mechanisms in place to share the data collected with the right people within their firms. Market research done properly is about more than just gathering data. It is also necessary to use the data.

MARKETING METHODS

Because consulting is an individualized service based on personal contact, consultants have an opportunity to be quite creative in their marketing approaches. However, very few firms are innovative in their techniques. In fact, most consulting firms do not market themselves very well at all. Perhaps this is due to the perception that as "professionals" it is somehow demeaning for consultants to think of themselves as "marketers" or "salespeople." In fact, many firms have traditionally used terms like business development or practice development or relationship building as if to somehow hide the fact that they were engaged in marketing initiatives.

Regardless of what they may call it (a rose by any other name . . .), successful firms have learned to utilize a variety of techniques to bring in new business. Among the more common methods are:

Personal Contacts

Referrals

Speeches/Training Programs

Articles and Books

Research

Public Relations

Cold Calls

Advertising

Personal Contacts—Chances are that you know or can be introduced to people who are in need of consulting service. In fact, personal connections are the favored method for consultants to find clients, and for clients to select consultants. With the innumerable number of possible clients out there and their basic lack of knowledge of consulting firms, coupled with the limited marketing budgets of consulting firms, it's no wonder that personal contacts are the best way for consultants and clients to find out if they are right for each other.

As noted previously, the most profitable source of new business comes from having a good relationship with your existing clients who can give you additional business. The goal should be to develop an ever closer relationship with your clients. There are three good reasons for doing so:

1. The costs of prospecting are usually lower than for developing new clients.

2. Trust and confidence are key components in the selling of consulting services, so if you have already developed a relationship, the battle is partially won.

3. Clients are usually less sensitive about fees for follow-on work than for initial assignments.

It is no wonder that most of the consulting firms I have spoken with report that, on average, two-thirds of their business comes from existing clients and one-third from new clients. So how can you develop better relationships with your clients? Well, you can:

▲ Increase the amount and frequency of contact with your clients by phoning often, visiting regularly, introducing your firm's clients, and, to the greatest extent possible, get additional executives from the client organization involved in your project.

▲ Improve your personal relationship with the client by remembering the client's family, their names and important dates, by inviting the client to social and sporting events, and by making it easy for the client to get in touch with you.

▲ Develop the business by sending the client copies of articles of interest to the client, offering to put on a seminar or training program for client staff members, and/or offering to attend the client's company meetings.

As consulting firms come to realize the importance of their existing client base, some firms are assigning a senior level executive to serve as a "client relationship manager." Rather than just being concerned about a single project, a relationship manager is concerned about a particular client and all of the services provided or offered to that client.

Referrals—There are any number of potential sources for referrals; unfortunately, too many consulting firms do not tap into these sources very effectively. Referrals are often available from within your own firm, especially if your firm is larger and offers multiple services or works in several industries. At first glance, this type of referral would seem to be obvious. And independent consulting firms often look accusingly (and probably longingly) at the big accounting firms for the amount of business that their consulting arms could receive from referrals from the tax and audit sides. In reality, however, cross-referral and cross-selling are more matters of wishful thinking in most firms than they are large revenue generators. Some of the reasons for this will be discussed later in this chapter.

Referrals can come from other consulting and professional service firms. Many consulting firms have established formal and informal networks with other consulting and even accounting, law, public relations, and advertising firms for the express purpose of referring business back and forth in non-competing practice areas. In addition, don't overlook your own firm's outside advisors who might be able to refer your firm to some of their other clients.

Your firm's board of directors can also be a source of referrals. Many consulting firms have business executives, academics, and others who often have their own extensive networks of people, some of whom could potentially become your clients.

Likewise, your clients can provide you with referrals. In some cases your clients' CEOs or other senior officers may serve on the boards of other companies and can share information about you with their colleagues from other industries. Remember, though, if they are not satisfied with your work, they will also let that be known.

Active membership and participation in trade and professional associations can result in referrals. Both ACME and the Institute of Management Consultants have referral systems whereby their members are referred to prospective clients. And your firm should be active and visible in the associations where your clients and desired clients are members. Many of these groups have their own referral systems or publish "buyer's guides" to help their members locate consultants.

And don't forget about suppliers as sources of referrals. Many of the "Big 6" accounting firms and other large IT consulting firms have relationships with computer hardware and software manufacturers which generate a number of opportunities. Depending on the nature of your business, there may be opportunities for you as well with such diverse entities as banks, insurance companies, construction firms, logistics and warehouse equipment manufacturers, shipping and transportation companies, etc.

Speeches—Presenting at seminars can help to position you as an expert, enhances your visibility, and allows you to interact with prospective clients in a professional setting. The key, of course, is to follow up after the conference (assuming of course you did a good job with your presentation). If you can get a copy of the registration list from the seminar sponsor, your follow-up is made easier. If not, it is up to you to collect business cards by directly asking for them, or by offering to send something (an article, a copy of your speech, etc.) to those who turn in their business card.

An alternative, of course, is for your consulting firm to host its own seminars. By doing so, you get to control the attendance and the agenda and to present yourself and your firm as "experts" on the topic(s) for your choice. To be successful, however, the seminar must be of value to those you invite and have something new to say. Some firms have been so successful in the area of hosted seminars and training programs that, not only are they able to use them to introduce their new products and services, seminars and training programs have actually become profit centers for the firms.

Articles and Books—Being a published author provides you with heightened credibility and keeps your name in front of prospective clients even when you are not there. The best and most effective articles are those which position you as a "thought leader" and which makes the reader want to get in touch with you. Some larger firms (such as McKinsey, A.D. Little, Booz-Allen, etc.) even publish and distribute their own high quality magazines which they feel are helpful in their prospective efforts; they give

Problem-Solver 4-2
MAKING BETTER PRESENTATIONS

The Issue

I am not comfortable speaking in front of a group. What can I do to make sure I reach my audience?

Let's Work This Through

As a consultant, you are often going to be called upon to address groups of people: speeches, sales presentations, proposal explanations, final reports. If it is any consolation, most people hate to speak in public. But there are some ways to help your audience to remember your message.

1. People remember the first and last things you say. Put your most important points up front and drive them home.

2. Audiences absorb as little as 25% of what you are saying. Be clear, logical, succinct, and repeat your message.

3. Attention spans are short, so don't get bogged down in extraneous detail. Make every sentence count.

4. People retain visual information. Paint pictures with your words in vibrant language.

5. First impressions are difficult to change. Look, act, and speak like a confident professional.

6. Research shows that your message is conveyed: 7% through words; 38% through your vocal inflection; and 55% through body signals. Rehearse not just words, but your voice and actions.

7. Never read your presentation to the audience. 93% of your message is non-verbal. Eye contact, smiles, and natural gestures help to make the audience like you.

8. Don't try to be who you're not. Let your own personality shine through rather than trying to copy another speaker.

9. Make sure your audio-visuals are of top caliber, and use them properly and effectively.

10. Practice Q&A in advance. Ask some of your colleagues to come up with some questions your presentation is likely to generate. Ask yourself ten questions you would hate to get. Fashion your answers in advance.

the marketing team something to talk about, and they differentiate the firm from its competition.

Articles can be reprinted and handed out at speeches and conferences; reprints can also be mailed to your present and prospective clients, and they can be sent to people who call you to ask if you have expertise in a particular area. Well done articles can be effective marketing tools for many years.

So if articles and books (though they may not be read by as large an audience as an article, they allow you to say that your firm "wrote the book on the subject") are so valuable, why don't more firms use them? The answer lies in the fact that writing takes time and discipline. Successful firms have learned, however, that the effort is more than justified by the rewards.

Research—Information and data provide the basis for seminars, articles, and books. The depth and breadth of the research can vary from major, global studies to relatively simple opinion surveys of what a particular group thinks about a given subject. Research does not have to cost a lot of money to generate a lot of publicity for your firm. There is usually a great deal of interest about business-related issues, so the business media is frequently looking for material.

Research conducted on topics of interest to your clients increases your value to your clients by helping them and you to stay abreast of emerging trends in their industry. The main thing is to provide your clients with information they cannot readily get from other sources. You want to be able to distinguish yourself as a resource your client needs. The information collected could be technical or professional in nature (new products, standards, techniques, etc.) or it could be somewhat more general, such as a survey of industry CEOs on their most pressing problems, the solutions they have attempted, and a ranking of the effectiveness of the various techniques. While research of this type may not result in "breakthrough thinking," it is of value to your clients because it can help them compare their company to their competition, and may save them time and money.

Many consulting firms have been successful in getting trade or professional associations to "partner" with the firm on research projects. In some cases the association may even underwrite or sponsor the financing of the research, but just getting the association's name affiliated with yours lends an aura of credibility to your firm.

Conducting research for use in articles and books can also be used as a technique for getting you in front of prospective clients. Senior executives who may not otherwise be accessible to you for a "sales call" may be willing to meet with you if the purpose of your visit (or phone call) is to interview them as part of your research for an article. Be honest, however, if you do get to meet or talk to them. Limit the discussion to the gathering of research information. Don't try to turn the opportunity into a sales call unless the other person invites you to do so by asking you for specific information about your firm. For now, it is simply enough to have had the chance to meet or talk.

And always offer to send the executive a copy of your article or relevant portions of the manuscript prior to submitting it for publication so he can review any quotes attributed to him for accuracy. This gives you a second opportunity to establish contact, and a third chance is provided to get your name in front of the prospective client when you send him a copy or reprint of the published article or book. The more familiar your name is to the prospect, the greater the chance you have of winding up with a new client.

Public Relations—Because PR is an indirect approach to generating publicity, the efforts can take a long time before any results are felt. But because references to your firm and its capabilities are presented in ways that do not appear to be blatant or self-serving, the impact on prospective clients can be very effective. Bear in mind,

Problem-Solver 4-3
PACKAGING YOUR MESSAGE

The Issue

How can I get the biggest bang-for-the-buck from my public relations program?

Let's Work This Through

According to John Bliss, founding partner of the public relations firm Bliss, Gouveneur & Associates, the key is to focus your message and then recycle it through several communications vehicles. That is, decide on what you want to say, and then write books and articles about the topic, speak about it, write editorials about it, give interviews about it, etc.

As for getting people interested in your message in a way that will bring you business, John recommends that you follow the 4P's:

1. Predictive—Make predictions based on your knowledge and expertise.

2. Prescriptive—What should people do based on your predictions.

3. Provocative—Be different in your message and your approach.

4. Prudent—Don't throw bombs unnecessarily; it may get you noticed, but it won't get you business.

In effect, consultants market predictable outcomes based on experience leading to new insights and ideas.

however, that just because you send out press releases, those to whom they are sent are under no obligation to use them. Many, if not most, press releases find their way into trash cans. And if your "news" is picked up for use in an article or news story, there is no guarantee that it will necessarily always be used in a favorable context. Many recent newspaper and magazine articles have been quite unflattering toward the consulting profession. You do not control the agenda or thrust of the story. However, a well-planned, pro-active public relations effort can help to position you as a resource for journalists who may respond by placing you in a more favorable light in their articles.

Public relations efforts can and should be a key component of a consulting firm's marketing efforts. As such, it requires time and effort and is worth paying attention to. But far too many firms do not do a very good job of managing or monitoring the quality and/or efficacy of their PR campaign. In fact, many firms fail to see public relations activities as a campaign, but rather tend to think of PR more in terms of either "damage control" (i.e., trying to put a positive "spin" on a negative occurrence) or as a means of announcing a special event. Some highly successful consulting firms, such as Andersen Consulting and Mercer, recognize the importance of public relations and have hired PR professionals to head up the firm's internal public relations department and/or to manage the activities of an external public relations firm hired by the consulting firm. In today's competitive marketplace, PR cannot be thought of as something a secretary does in his or her spare time.

Cold Calls—The thought of "pounding the pavement" and "banging on doors" in an attempt to sell consulting services is enough to give some consulting purists apoplexy. Cold calling has traditionally been thought of in terms of the door-to-door selling of products like encyclopedias, vacuum cleaners, and magazine subscriptions, not as a means of marketing professional services. Nevertheless, more and more frequently I run into consulting firms who utilize professional sales people and even telemarketers to set up appointments for the firm's executives to get in front of prospective clients. I am not intending to conjure up images of a van-load of nattily attired and carefully groomed executive-type people being set loose upon an industrial or business park with order books in hand, methodically ringing all the doorbells. But where careful prior research has been done on the prospective client, then a carefully crafted call to arrange a customized, face-to-face meeting can be quite successful.

Advertising—When I first joined the staff of the association of management consulting firms, there was a provision in its Code of Ethics which prohibited its members from advertising. At that time, consulting firms felt advertising was not only somehow "unprofessional" but a waste of money. Over the past 20 years, of course, the Code of Ethics has been revised to remove the restrictions on advertising (due in no small part to a U.S. Supreme Court ruling guaranteeing the professional the right to advertise), but debates about the cost effectiveness of advertising by consulting firms continue.

Opponents argue that advertising is an expensive means of reaching a large audience that does not buy consulting services out of a magazine or from a telephone number on their television screen. Proponents (the largest of which is Andersen Consulting, which not only advertises during televised golf matches, but has gone so far as to sponsor its own major tournament) counter that such activities afford the firm increased visibility (on a world-wide basis in the case of the Andersen Consulting World Championship of Golf), and enhanced relationships with its clients and potential clients.

If you do decide to engage in an advertising campaign, make sure you do some careful advance planning and research to ensure that your ads are placed where your clients and prospects are most likely to see them. Find out what magazines, newspapers, and trade publications your target audience reads. Understand specifically who you want to reach and what message you want to leave them with as a result of their having seen your ad. How will you get them to take the time to look at, much less read, watch, or listen to your ad? Some firms use humor, others play on the concerns of their target audience, others provide an answer to a commonly asked question, and still others rely on captivating graphics to grab attention.

Also when thinking about the use of advertising as a marketing technique, bear in mind the old but nonetheless very true adage, "Repetition makes reputation." A

Problem-Solver 4-4
DIRECT MAIL

The Issue

Does direct mail work for marketing consulting services?

Let's Work This Through

The quick answer is anything will work some of the time. Direct mail can at least set the stage by introducing your firm to a prospective client who might then be more open to taking your follow-up phone call.

The critical elements of direct mail are:

40%—The strength of your list of target opportunities.

40%—The message or offer.

20%—The package (creative, attention-grabbing).

When thinking about direct mail, remember the acronym AIDA—Attention Interest Desire Action.

one-time shot at advertising is not an efficient use of your money, even if you do mail out copies of the ad or the whole magazine to your target audience after the ad appears. With advertising, as with PR, be prepared to hang in there for the long term.

In addition to the marketing methods listed above, there are other activities some firms engage in which are worth considering, such as: becoming involved in community and civic groups; cultivating clients at social or sporting events; direct mail campaigns; and publishing and distributing newsletters.

Of course, any and all of these techniques can work and will work sometimes. We have all heard the stories of the contracts brought in as a result of a golf match or ball game. Community involvement can help you meet people, and as long as your newsletter can avoid becoming simply a repository for generic information, your target audience may find it of enough interest to read.

Different marketing methods are important to have, but there must be a coordinated, planned approach to using them aimed at a targeted audience if your marketing efforts are going to really be successful.

STRATEGIC POSITIONING OPTIONS

Deciding how your firm is going to compete is an important prelude to designing your market plan. How your firm is going to be positioned determines to a large extent who you will compete against and even what you are going to market. There are several different strategic positioning options used by consulting firms. These include:

▲ The focus of the firm, i.e., the firm concentrates on the services it will offer, the customers it will target, and/or the geographic market it serves.

▲ The firm can use its own image as a sales tool.

▲ The firm can compete on the basis of providing superior quality and consistency.

▲ The firm can market its ability to provide other services or products in addition to its consulting services.

▲ Low price relative to the value of services offered is another competitive position the firm can take.

Your firm's approach to positioning must be an integral component of both your strategic and market plans. I have found examples of successful firms which compete on the basis of each of the options listed above. Consistency of message is the key.

MARKETING ADVICE

The following is a compilation of advice I have gleaned in my years as a consultant and as an advisor to consulting firms.

▲ Walk the talk—Be and act like you are what you say you are. Establish the values of your firm, live up to those values, and instill them in your staff.

▲ Proper positioning—Determine the strategic positioning of your firm in accordance with your firm's values, and build your marketing efforts around that positioning.

▲ Credible claims—Be honest and believable in stating what your firm can and cannot do. A good rule of thumb is to treat every client project as though it were going to appear in tomorrow's newspaper, or you were going to have to defend your position in court.

▲ Consistent message—Make sure all your supporting materials convey the image you want to have for your firm.

▲ Establish an identity—"Build a better mousetrap, and the world will beat a path to your door," goes the old saying, but only if the world knows you built it and where you live. Clients have to know that your firm exists before they can hire your firm. Develop and promote a consistent corporate identity. Also make sure that the logo, typeface, etc. is similar on all of your promotional materials rather than looking like you just threw a variety of pieces together.

▲ Develop relationships—Don't sell products. Because consultants are often privy to the innermost operations of client organizations, the client must trust the consultant, and trust is built on relationships, not on products. An analogy to keep in mind in your marketing efforts is, "Tell the customer about the lawn he can have, not about your grass seed." Help the client envision the benefits he will derive rather than focusing on the product you're selling.

▲ Listen, don't tell—The client wants you to solve his problem and to understand his concerns. You can do this only by listening to the client rather than talking about your pre-packaged solutions or pre-conceived notions. This is often a difficult balance, because consultants want to demonstrate that they have had relevant prior experience and that they can come up with creative ways to answer the client's needs. Doing so, however, can often result in your "giving away the store."

▲ Customer testimonials work—It is one thing to say good things about yourself; however, they are much more believable and effective when someone else says them. Granted, many of your customers may not want you to use their names, but you won't know unless you ask.

▲ Establish and follow a marketing/sales sequence:

　▲ develop an understanding of the full extent of the client's need/problem.

　▲ establish and help the client see the full cost to the client of not meeting the need/problem.

　▲ demonstrate your ability to meet the need/problem.

　▲ establish and help the client see the cost/payoff equation.

▲ Manage non-billable staff time—Monitor how your consultants use their time when they are not working on and billing for client projects. Make sure they use this time in ways that will benefit the firm, such as on marketing-related activities or professional development initiatives.

10 TECHNIQUES TO GET MORE BUSINESS

1. *Determine who you want as clients and contact them.* Repeatedly send them useful information about their industry's issues or their specific problems, along with a personalized letter.

2. *Do excellent work.* Exceed the expectations of your current clients and encourage them to refer you to their customers, suppliers, and corporate friends.

3. *Develop case histories of your success stories.* Identify the problem you solved and how you solved it, and send these case histories for use as articles or sidebars to editors of publications read by your target audience.

4. *Be visible.* Write articles, give speeches, get interviewed, teach courses, attend and participate in trade and professional associations, etc.

5. *Stay in touch with prospective, former, and present clients.* Publish a newsletter filled with genuinely valuable information and helpful analysis. Strive for four to six issues a year to keep your name in front of your clients.

6. *Develop and use networks.* Participate in professional, service, social, and community organizations. Get involved and become known in associations of other management consultants—they can often be a good source of referrals, and other members might become strategic alliance candidates.

7. *Conduct a self-assessment.* Analyze your firm's strengths and weaknesses and those of your top competitors. Determine how you can capitalize on your strengths and overcome your weaknesses so you will be able and ready to answer questions your prospective clients might raise.

8. *Differentiate your firm.* Brainstorm with your staff consultants, clients, suppliers, friends, etc. and try to develop a list of 50 reasons why you should be the consultants they hire. Pay particular attention to everything that makes you different from your competition, and decide how best to capitalize on these differences.

9. *Use advertising if you can afford to.* It's expensive, but advertising works if you want to reach large groups of people repeatedly. Remember, "repetition makes reputation"—advertising is not cost-effective as a one-time event.

10. *Budget for marketing.* Business development requires time, effort, money, and management; successful firms budget and plan accordingly.

SALES—THE OBJECTIVE OF MARKETING

At their most basic levels, the difference between marketing and sales can be explained as follows:

Marketing	Sales
Firm capabilities	Make contacts
Market definition	Identify opportunities
Target clients	Gain interest
Pre-sales research	Develop proposal
Team coordination	Present proposal
Promotional efforts	Close sale
Sales tools	Monitor quarterly
Proposal support	Obtain follow-on

Marketing can get you in front of a prospect; selling turns that prospect into a client. It has been a common misconception, however, that consultants don't have to sell. Nothing could be farther from the truth. Consulting success requires constant selling. You sell yourself to a firm to get hired as a consultant, you sell yourself to get assigned to projects, you sell yourself and your firm to bring in new business, sell continuously to your present clients so that they will remain your clients, and then sell to them again to get follow-on work.

It is also true that most consultants I have interviewed don't like to sell. They are, after all, "professionals," which evokes a belief that those in need of the services of a professional should be the ones to seek out the service provider. Then, too, most consultants enter the field because they want to solve problems and use their technical skills, not to become salespeople. The idea of selling seems to be somehow "beneath" them. This perception is carried over into the professional development programs of many consulting firms where sales training is perfunctory at best, if offered at all. Then, too, most consulting firms promote people based on their technical knowledge and problem-solving skills. But once those employees approach partnership levels, they are suddenly expected to bring in significant amounts of new business. And unless they can demonstrate sales abilities, not only will they not be promoted to partner, their future employment with the firm may be at risk. The truth of the matter is, to succeed in consulting, you have to be able to sell.

STRATEGIC SELLING

A key concept in marketing services today is that of strategic selling. As with most phrases or techniques in the world of consulting, the term "strategic selling" can mean different things to different people. Here are some of the components I think about when discussing the idea:

- ▲ What do you want to sell? A project? A series of projects? An ongoing relationship? You have to know what your ultimate goal is in advance of going to market with your services.

- ▲ What particular needs of your prospective client are you going to meet? Analyze the specific needs of each individual prospect and how you are going to address that need.

- ▲ Understand and acknowledge the importance of:
  - ▲ Attitudes of the prospective customer.
  - ▲ Demographics which indicate what people do.
  - ▲ Psychographics which indicate why they do it.

- ▲ Spend more time analyzing what works in your sales presentations and why it works and less time worrying about what doesn't work.

▲ Sell the client on how they will benefit from your services rather than high-lighting the features of your offering.

▲ Understand and capitalize on your firm's positioning, i.e., who you are, how the market perceives you, the perception you generate by the types of affiliations you have, and the endorsements you receive.

▲ Present and former satisfied clients are always your best market opportunities.

THE SALES PROCESS

Selling requires learnable skills such as active listening, asking the right questions, persuading, negotiating, presenting, and closing. The sales process overlaps with the marketing process in some respects in that they both seek to: (1) establish rapport between you and the prospect; (2) help you obtain information about the needs of the prospective client; (3) provide you with an opportunity to share information about your firm; (4) help the prospect to see that your firm has the ability to meet the needs of the client; and (5) anticipate and respond to concerns and objections of the prospect.

There are many books available which can help you to hone your selling skills, so instead of rehashing them here, I would like to share with you the following information which comes from a training program used by one of the larger consulting firms to help its consultants understand the sales process:

▲ Opening the door

    ▲ Third party introductions (friends, staff members, board members, other professionals, vendors, etc.)

    ▲ Meetings, meals, conferences, followed by a telephone call

    ▲ Letter followed by a call.

    ▲ Cold telephone call with a "hook"

▲ Get a meeting

    ▲ Decide purpose/direction

    ▲ Informal or business setting

    ▲ Number of consulting firm attendees

    ▲ Do your homework, learn about the company and the company employees who will attend meeting

▲ Always confirm the meeting

▲ Decide which consulting firm employees will play what role

▲ Role-play and rehearse before the meeting

▲ The first meeting

  ▲ Dress appropriately

  ▲ Be early

  ▲ Be friendly to the receptionist and secretary

  ▲ Assess the setting

  ▲ Know the tools you have available

  ▲ Have opening ready

  ▲ Be mentally prepared

  ▲ Don't use "sir" or "ma'am"

▲ In informal settings

  ▲ Be sociable and personal

  ▲ Ask questions

  ▲ Pay attention to the client

  ▲ Lead the discussion to your firm

  ▲ Tell "war stories"

  ▲ Request a formal meeting

  ▲ End on a personal note

▲ In formal settings

  ▲ Determine time available

  ▲ Allow "get to know each other" discussion

  ▲ Pay attention and speak to everyone present

  ▲ Ask questions

  ▲ Listen/be sensitive to what is going on

  ▲ Protect the client's pride/"face"

  ▲ Provide "free" advice

▲ Surface opportunities where you can help

  ▲ What are three major challenges the client faces?

  ▲ How does client compare to industry peers?

▲ Respond with your experiences

▲ Offer "pluses" of hiring your firm

▲ Determine "buy" guidelines

▲ Budgetary restrictions

▲ Competition/selection criteria

▲ Expectations

▲ Approval "chain"/decision process

▲ Talk about teaming with client

▲ Emphasize that you are the "right" firm

▲ Be aware of traps

▲ Industry problems

▲ Client "ego"

▲ Competition's "edge"/"wired" projects

▲ "Low ball" quotes

▲ Don't knock your competitor

▲ Create confidence in you and your firm

▲ Have a strong closing

▲ Summarize the discussion

▲ Offer something: next meeting, reprints, newsletters, proposal draft, etc.

▲ Say "Thank You" for the time, interest, etc.

▲ Proposal Preparation

▲ Match with client's needs/wants

▲ Appearance of work is important

▲ Use "creative" approaches

▲ Adjust scope if pricing is a problem

▲ Quality control—check spelling/names

▲ Emphasize end-products/results

▲ Adhere to your firm's proposal process

▲ Delivering the Proposal

▲ In person (unless prohibited)

▲ Bring project manager in to meet client

  ▲ Mark "draft" so changes can be made

  ▲ Negotiate by reducing scope

  ▲ Gain support/commitment

  ▲ Set start date or get decision date

  ▲ Close with "Is there anything else?"

▲ Follow-On Work

  ▲ Opportunity for cross-selling

  ▲ Be alert/sensitive to other needs

  ▲ Read client planning documents

  ▲ Expand inside contacts/supporters

  ▲ Talk about other assignments of your firm

  ▲ Become a "personal advisor" to the client

Problem-Solver 4-5
FOLLOW-UP

The Issue

How can I become more successful at selling?

Let's Work This Through

On the whole, 98% of all sales are not made on the first call. In fact, on average you have to call on a prospect five to ten times before the first sale is made. Therefore, follow-up is an absolute requirement.

Get to know the prospect's "hot buttons"—things or issues that will make him or her buy. Then make sure that each time you follow up, you give the prospect new information that hits those hot buttons. Finally, be prepared for anything, so be flexible enough in your follow-up approach to listen for and address new information.

Here are some questions to ask yourself about how you follow up:

1. Am I sincere in my desire to help the client first and put the sale second?

2. Am I funny? People love to laugh. A laughing prospect is more likely to buy.

3. Am I direct in my communication?

4. Am I friendly? People buy from friends, not from salespeople.

5. Am I selling benefits and telling the prospect how he will benefit from my services?

▲   Ask for referrals

▲   Know client's budget/timing

▲   Brainstorm about opportunities with your staff members

Regardless of the books you read or the strategy or process you employ, there are a few key points to remember when talking about selling and the consulting business:

1. If you want to survive, you've got to sell.

2. No matter how busy you are on project work, you've got to make time to sell.

3. You are responsible for developing your own ability to sell.

4. Strive to enjoy the selling part of the job as much as the consulting side.

5. Sales is a numbers game. Just like Babe Ruth, you are going to strike out more frequently than you will hit a home run. The key is to keep trying.

CROSS-SELLING—AN ELUSIVE GOAL

As noted earlier in this chapter, many consulting organizations would appear on the surface to have significant opportunities to develop large amounts of new business simply on the basis of one group or part of the firm being able to refer work to other divisions. The "Big 6" firms come immediately to mind with their well-entrenched audit partners feeding leads and work to the consulting groups. In theory, it seems like a clear-cut competitive advantage; in practice it is rarely that easy. In my interviews with dozens of consulting firms, there have been many reasons offered as to why cross-selling fails to live up to its potential, including:

▲ Partners or practice areas already having a relationship with a client don't want to jeopardize that relationship by bringing in another practice area which may not be able to solve the client's problem or in some other manner do something which could anger or alienate the client.

▲ Those persons responsible for business development in one area are often too busy with their own responsibilities to have time to look for opportunities for another group.

▲ Practice managers tend to wear "blinders" and can only see or hear opportunities for their own areas, and are frequently not even aware of all the practice areas their firm is engaged in.

▲ Unless tied directly to compensation schemes, most firms offer no incentives to those bringing in business outside of their own practice area or line of business.

A few firms, however, have been able to overcome these obstacles to cross-selling. Here are some of their secrets:

▲ Education and reinforcement of the importance of cross-selling to the firm's culture and to the consultant's future with the firm must begin upon employment and continue throughout their time with the firm.

▲ Tracking and disseminating information about all of the firm's assignments and capabilities of the firm's staff is crucial. An individual must be designated and given both the responsibility and the authority to function as the firm's "knowledge development officer."

▲ Running in-house seminars to teach networking skills.

▲ Use of teleconferences to share information among and between offices and practice areas about the types of clients and assignments different groups are seeking.

▲ Assigning a "Client Relationship Manager" to each major client. This person is responsible for making sure that the client is kept happy as well as informing the client about all of the firm's lines of business which are available to meet the diverse needs of that client.

The most successful consulting firms have been able to convince their staffs that they are part of a team, not a group of individuals, and that when the team wins, they all win.

60 SUCCESSFUL MARKETING IDEAS

In marketing, the recipe for success includes a variety of ingredients including: involving your clients and prospective clients, keeping aware of (and hopefully ahead of) your competition, constant innovation, and taking advantage of cross-selling opportunities. Here are five dozen marketing concepts, techniques, and strategies that really work:

1. *Position your services, products, expertise and your firm.* How do you want your prospective clients to think about your firm and its services? What does that prospect think about your competition? How can you break through the

idea that "consultants are all the same" and differentiate your firm in the mind of the buyer? How can you establish yourself as the "first one that comes to mind" when prospective clients think about consulting firms? There are many books and articles available about positioning—find them, read them, and put their ideas to work.

2. *Involve the client.* Use every opportunity to stay in touch with your clients. Present clients are your best source for uncovering and finding what your prospective clients are likely to need. Use the information to refine your marketing program. Every time one of your consultants talks to a client it is a fact-finding and marketing opportunity. Also, don't forget to survey clients at the conclusion of each engagement. Not only will the results help you to refine your future marketing activities, but they may uncover opportunities for add-on services with the client who is responding to the survey.

3. *Use your firm's best selling services/products to help sell other activities.* Don't be afraid to "ride the coattail" of your most popular services. If you consult on strategy, use your expertise to sell implementation and training programs. If you offer systems integration, use it to open the door for change management. Think about the broader needs of the client from the client's perspective.

4. *Understand the difference between marketing and sales.* Marketing is primarily foundational in nature. It includes the work you do to understand customers and markets, and to match services and products to identified needs. Sales is the implementation of marketing initiatives. Both marketing and sales are crucial to success.

5. *Constantly innovate and develop your services and products so they provide benefits to clients.* You can't afford to sit still, In the words of Will Rogers, "Even if you're on the right track, you can get run over when the train comes through." If you don't take the time to improve your offerings, someone else will. Real profits lie in improving and customizing since the hardest work and highest costs are in developing your offerings and establishing them in the marketplace.

6. *Track everything you do and analyze what you've done.* Learn from both your successes and your failures. Determine what types of marketing activities and materials work best for your firm and your target market. Find out how prospective clients first heard about your firm.

7. *Practice client-savvy, client-driven, not product- or service-driven marketing.* Build your marketing and sales efforts around what your clients need, not around what you have to sell.

8. *Identify client needs through market research.* Use feedback mechanisms and meetings to identify issues of concern to your clients. If you don't have good market research capabilities in-house, contract it out.

9. *Provide exceptional service and value.* Client loyalty is built on value and service, not on price. Delivering more than the client expected turns the client into an advocate.

10. *Know who your clients are.* Understand and target your marketing efforts at the right people at the right level in the right companies, i.e., those who actually buy your services. A fancy campaign aimed at the CEO might make you feel good, but it won't result in any business if it is the CIO or VP of Manufacturing, etc., who makes the decision whether to hire your firm or not. Develop profiles on your targeted clients and determine their interests, needs, purchasing process, and key decision makers.

11. *Never lose a client or proposal without finding out why.* Turn negative events into learning experiences so you can do better in the future. Don't be afraid to ask "Why?" You may learn some very helpful information about your firm and/or your competition.

12. *Monitor and understand the trends impacting your firm, the consulting profession, and your clients.* Many firms at least try to keep abreast of changes and trends that their clients are confronting. Successful firms also realize that the consulting profession itself is undergoing change. These firms participate in organizations such as ACME and the Institute of Management Consultants to share information and learn from their peers.

13. *Integrate your services and products into a single marketing function.* Let the marketplace see all of the services your firm has to offer. A unified marketing approach also helps your staff with cross-selling.

14. *Cultivate prior clients.* Don't forget about past clients. They may have new needs you can meet, so you may be able to generate new business from them directly, or by keeping your name in front of them, they are more likely to think of you when they are asked for referrals.

15. *Market relationships rather than selling projects.* Invest in the time and technology to build up-to-date databases which permit you to identify and qualify prospective clients and then focus and target your marketing efforts on understanding and meeting the specific needs of each prospect.

16. *Keep an eye on the calendar.* Marketing campaigns require paying attention to timing. Understanding your client's and prospect's budgeting cycle lets you

time your proposal to arrive just before the process begins. Timing is also important in following up when you said you would.

17. *Target your mailings.* Mailings can keep your name in front of prospects and clients, but the materials they receive must be relevant to them or you will be sending the wrong message. Keep your mailing lists up-to-date as well. Mail sent to the wrong person or wrong address is unprofessional.

18. *Create awareness through sponsorship.* You may not be in the same league as Andersen Consulting which sponsored The World Championship of Golf and other major events. But you can sponsor or host cocktail parties or other activities at a trade association meeting where your clients and prospects will be in attendance. Or how about an exhibit or booth at a trade show? The key is to build name recognition.

19. *Write articles highlighting success stories about your services.* Develop articles for both your in-house publications and for dissemination to external media. Don't assume that other staff members in your firm are aware of what you're doing. Keep them (as well as your clients and prospects) informed.

20. *Plan the timing of your mail delivery.* Mail on Monday or Tuesday so the mail arrives later in the week when there is traditionally less volume. Your mailing has a better chance of being read if there is less competition.

21. *Develop a list of all the services and products offered by your firm.* Ask each partner, department head, etc. to contribute to a master list of everything your firm offers. Such a list is invaluable in writing marketing copy and for identifying cross-selling opportunities.

22. *Listen when clients call to help identify needs.* Determine what people are asking for by paying attention to and tracking incoming calls. If you find a significant number are inquiries about a product or service, consider expanding your visibility in that area if it is something you presently offer, or explore the feasibility of developing a capability in the area if you don't presently offer it.

23. *Remind yourself and your staff what business you're really in.* Generally speaking, consulting firms are in the business of helping clients solve problems. This implies an attitude of service, that the client really does come first.

24. *Use focus groups and follow up.* Focus groups can be very helpful in developing new approaches, techniques, practices, etc. If you use focus groups, however, don't forget to follow up with the participants regarding the outcome. They want to feel that they made a difference, and it is a way for you to generate a greater sense of commitment to your firm.

25. *Prepare a written plan for every marketing initiative.* A plan keeps you from simply focusing on the easy stuff. Putting it in writing lets all of your staff know what you're trying to do and how they can help.

26. *Commit to client satisfaction.* Position your firm as a quality provider dedicated to keeping clients happy. Remember that a satisfied client is your best form of advertisement and can be an adjunct to your sales force.

27. *Bundle your offerings.* Develop tailored bundles or packages of services you can offer to meet the specific needs of individual clients. Let them know all the ways you can be of service to them.

28. *Add value rather than cutting price.* It's a competitive market, and you will be pressured to lower price. Don't do it. Once you do, your professional service becomes a commodity. Demonstrate all the extra benefits and value the client will receive from your efforts in excess of the proposed costs. If the client still says the price is too high, offer to narrow the scope of the project as a way of bringing the cost down rather than discounting your prices.

29. *Know your competition.* Take time to find out as much as you can about your competition, including products, practice areas, strategy, objectives, pricing, etc. See how they service their clients and what they are developing as new markets.

30. *Let your clients know what's in it for them.* Clients want to know what they are going to get for their money. They may think you're wonderful, but they still want to know "What's in it for me?" Develop a market plan from the perspective of the client.

31. *Establish realistic and measurable goals.* Impossible goals and unrealistic expectations will kill your best marketers. Don't do that. Make goals measurable so you can track success.

32. *Communicate value and service.* If you're good, let the world know. If you don't tell your story, no one else will do it for you.

33. *Set time limits for your proposals to remain in effect.* Let prospects know that the terms, conditions, and prices quoted in your proposal will remain in effect for a certain period of time (usually 30 days). You may prevent an awkward situation of a prospective client trying to hold you to old prices.

34. *Don't underprice.* Your price should reflect the quality of your services. Many of your clients may adhere to the adage, "You get what you pay for."

35. *Cross-sell.* Never miss an opportunity to let a client know all of the capabilities of your firm. Cross-selling is a low-cost way to expand your business and to build client loyalty.

36. *Do your selling in the cover letter.* Target the letter to the specific audience, and let them know how you are going to meet their needs and the benefits they will derive. Don't write an "enclosed is a brochure" style form letter.

37. *Use testimonials.* Using testimonials from satisfied clients adds interest and credibility to your marketing efforts.

38. *Make it easy for your clients to reach you.* Include telephone, 800, fax, and e-mail numbers of your firm on all correspondence. Don't assume people have your data on file.

39. *Allocate resources properly.* Line up your resources before beginning a marketing initiative. If you sign up clients and can't service them properly or in a timely manner, you will not only lose them, you will turn them into detractors.

40. *Establish a corporate identity.* Strong and consistent graphics are essential to your firm's success. You need pieces that contribute to building a strong, recognizable identity for your firm in the marketplace.

41. *Create events.* If one of your consultants writes a book, create a media-covered book signing event. Sponsor symposia, workshops, breakfast, lunch, or dinner meetings. Bring in outside speakers and invite clients to attend a presentation/reception. Create opportunities for people to talk about your firm.

42. *Use a postscript (P.S.).* People will read it. Make sure it has a powerful selling message.

43. *Develop and distribute a publication.* Newsletters, magazines, journals, etc., if done properly, can be excellent marketing tools. Include articles by people outside of your firm to enhance credibility.

44. *Send fax reminders of your events.* They serve as last-minute marketing opportunities, and you can generally increase attendance at your events.

45. *Acknowledge every client contact.* Thank-you notes are the least expensive form of public relations between you and your clients. Accept no excuses or delays in acknowledging every meeting or contact with a client or prospect.

46. *Constantly measure your success.* Track every marketing initiative and sale. Build a database of what works and doesn't work based on facts, not suppositions.

47. *Cut mailing costs while adding value.* Tailor your mailings to the needs of each prospect or client rather than sending out large packets of generic information.

48. *Say thank you.* It never hurts to keep thanking the client. Let them know that you appreciate their business, and they are more likely to want to do business with you again.

49. *Use newsletters as marketing and sales tools.* Prepare a newsletter that's full of good and useful information. Within the body of the newsletter, position columns that sell your services and products. Be sure that your sales pitch is germane to the article in which it is positioned.

50. *Set up a fax-on-demand system.* Offer a fax-on-demand and/or an on-line system to make it easy for clients to obtain information about your firm. Include in your offerings articles written by your staff members. Track requests for information so you can follow up.

51. *Concentrate on your areas of success.* Find your niche and fill it. Stake out your position so strongly that others can't compete effectively. You can't do it all, so focus on what you do most successfully.

52. *Take care of your staff.* Respect and treat your staff well, and they will treat your clients with respect. Don't just focus on your consulting staff. Remember that those who answer the telephone and support your consultants will also have contact with clients.

53. *Make it easy for clients to provide feedback.* Solicit feedback during and after each assignment. Let the client know that you listen to and act on his suggestions.

54. *Invest in customer service training.* Provide training for all those who will have client contact. Your investment will more than pay for itself in good client relationships, repeat business, and referrals.

55. *Stay close to your clients.* Never take a client for granted, even, or especially, if it has been a long-term client. Make a commitment to constantly strengthen relationships. Do research to keep in touch with the needs of your clients.

56. *Reward for repeat business.* Don't fall into the trap of rewarding those who bring in new clients while offering fewer or no incentives to those who develop repeat business from present clients. Encourage your staff to be alert for additional ways your firm can help the client.

57. *Investigate and evaluate joint ventures before jumping into them.* Joint marketing initiatives (such as co-sponsored seminars, etc.) between your firm and another firm or vendor can be effective, but do your homework in advance. Test the reputation of the other firm with the target audience for the program. Have any contracts reviewed by legal counsel before signing. Agree in advance on mailing lists and ownership of those lists, etc.

58. *Expand your reach through affiliations.* Formal and informal networking groups can introduce you to new opportunities.

59. *Respond promptly to complaints.* You can often turn a negative experience around by quickly responding to a complaint and getting the client who complained involved in developing a resolution.

60. *Reach for the sky sometimes.* Once in a while set an unrealistic goal. You may be surprised how close you can come to achieving it.

61. *Maintain high standards and ethics.* Quality is not enough. Clients must be able to trust you and the people who work for you. If you utilize associates or sub-contractors, select people with the same ethical standards as yours.

62. *Build strong relationships with clients.* A client is worth more than an individual project. Treat them as though your entire future depends on keeping them happy—it does.

63. *Delegate.* Just because you're the CEO doesn't mean you have to do or personally oversee everything. You'll drive yourself crazy if you try to, and you'll stifle the development of others.

64. *Always give more than the client expects.* In today's competitive marketplace, simply meeting expectations is not sufficient. If you promised ten benefits, give them more.

65. *Bear in mind that low-cost suppliers don't always deliver the best value.* Don't be "penny-wise and pound-foolish" when hiring outside resources such as public relations counsel, printers, etc. Your firm's image is at stake.

66. *Clients buy solutions, not products.* Market and sell benefits and solutions. Focus on relationships, not projects.

67. *Deliver more than you promise.* Remember, I offered you 60 tips, but delivered a bonus.

SOME FINAL THOUGHTS ABOUT MARKETING

While the nature of your consulting practice and your competition may determine precisely which marketing and sales approaches your firm utilizes, there are some generalities which seem to apply to most consulting firms. These include:

▲ There is no direct evidence that having a high-quality brochure outlining your firm's capabilities will gain you additional business, but when all of your competitors do have them, not having one can hurt you.

▲ Regardless of the size of your firm, you can't be all things to all people. It is necessary to define the market(s) you are going to concentrate on. Depending on the nature of your practice, you may define it by industry or by service offering, but remember, prospective clients want to hire specialists.

▲ Within your defined market, every company can be viewed as a prospective client, but some deserve special targeting for proactive sales efforts. Targets are usually selected based on: size (the company is the size that you are best able to serve); industry (where you have the greatest experience, or an industry you want to gain experience in); ability to pay (consultants are altruistic by nature, and often undertake pro-bono work, but remember, you still have a business to run); need/problem of the client is a match with your capabilities; management level (market to people who actually hire and/or work with you, not to the CEO just because it makes your ego feel good).

▲ After targeting a select group of companies to contact, research each specific company prior to contacting them directly. The more individualized you can make the sales contact, the greater your chances of making the sale.

▲ Marketing, sales, and project work are all team efforts, and it is important from the outset to coordinate these teams and to assign responsibilities for management.

▲ The primary purpose of a consulting firm's promotional efforts is to generate interest in and awareness of the firm among prospective clients. Promotional activities may not result in direct sales, but are used to obtain referrals, to gain intelligence about companies who might be interested in your services, to be asked to come in to a company to make a proposal, and to be introduced to company decision makers. Among the more common promotional activities used by consulting firms

---

Problem-Solver 4-6
ELEMENTS OF A PROPOSAL

The Issue

I've been asked to submit a written proposal by a prospective client. What do I need to cover?

Let's Work This Through

A good proposal that gives you a chance at getting a new client should include:

1. A statement of why the proposal is being submitted and a description of the work to be performed.

2. An indication of the timing of the work, the responsibility for accomplishing the work, and the cost of the work.

3. A summary of the benefits the client can expect.

---

are: making speeches at meetings where prospective clients are in attendance; writing articles to appear in publications read by clients; attending group meetings such as professional societies, trade associations, community groups, social settings, church activities, school groups, etc., and letting people know about you and your firm.

▲ Compiling, allocating, and managing the sales tools available to your consultants must be taken into consideration as part of your firm's marketing plan. Among the things firms include when talking about sales tools are: telephones, business cards, letters, brochures/surveys/reprints, lists of qualifications and references, "war stories," prior reports, client contact and confirmation cards, support of and access to partners and managers of the consulting firm, and the handling of expenses and reimbursements.

▲ Proposal support includes advance decisions on such matters as: will proposals be reviewed by legal counsel, proofreaders, central coordinator of proposals, etc., and who will handle typing, mailing, etc. Procedures must be in place before proposals are prepared.

Marketing, sales, technical competence, relationship building, and firm management are all vital components to Success In Consulting.

PREPARING PROPOSALS

If you've done a good job in marketing and selling your services, a prospective client may ask you to prepare a written proposal. A clearly defined proposal is more than a marketing tool, it can serve as the basis for planning and monitoring the engagement.

BEFORE PREPARING A PROPOSAL

After a client has expressed interest in having you submit a proposal, there are some things you should attempt to do before you sit down to begin writing. These include:

▲ Identifying where the prospective client is feeling discomfort and the source of that discomfort. For example, is the problem in the manufacturing area and is the cause of the problem actually in the manufacturing process, or is it that the company's sales people are selling the wrong thing or making unrealistic promises to customers?

▲ Ascertaining what the real need of the client is. Get behind the words the client is saying and try to discover what is really going on.

▲ Identifying the personal benefits the client is looking for as a result of bringing in a consultant.

▲ Talking to the client to get a handle on who in your firm is likely to have the best "chemistry" with the client. Plan on having this person involved in the presentation of your proposal.

▲ Working with the client to jointly define the problem you are being asked to address.

▲ Discovering the fee level the client expects to pay for the consulting engagement.

▲ Finding out what the client's time frame is for starting and completing the project.

▲ Learning who the real decision makers are at the company. It's not always the person with the most impressive title.

▲ Finding someone in the client organization who can serve as your "sponsor" or "champion" as a result of their commitment to wanting to solve the problem, or because they are familiar with your firm and the quality of your work.

▲ Getting the client to feel obligated to moving ahead on the project.

The foregoing activities are by-and-large things you need to get from the client prior to drafting a written proposal. There are also things you should do for yourself, such as:

▲ Meeting the key players from the client organization.

▲ Listening before speaking. Don't fall into the trap of trying to demonstrate how wonderful you and your firm are until the client has a chance to tell you what he is looking for.

▲ Getting emotionally involved in wanting to solve the client's problem. Successful projects are more than academic exercises.

▲ Thinking like your client and really try to understand them and their perception of the situation. Don't negate the importance of their problem, even if the problem doesn't seem that big or complicated to you.

▲ Saying "you" before "I" or "we." Speak to the client's needs and the benefits he will derive, not what we will offer as features.

▲ Assessing your competition and the strategy they are likely to employ in their proposals.

▲ Sticking to the issues so you don't appear to be on a fishing expedition when gathering information from the client.

▲ Communicating clearly with the prospect to reduce the likelihood of misunderstandings.

▲ Gently planting your firm's message in the mind of the prospective client.

▲ Being persistent, but not turning off the client. Let him know that you are thorough and that you follow up, but be careful not to be antagonistic or thought of as a "pest."

WHEN NOT TO SUBMIT PROPOSALS

Just because someone likes your marketing materials, it does not mean you have to or should submit a proposal to work for that person. That's why it is so important to try to meet the prospective client face-to-face before submitting a proposal rather than simply responding to a mail solicitation so you can establish a sense of "fit" between your firm's services and the client's needs.

Your goal should be to put time and effort into preparing a proposal only if there is a real chance that you can get the business. When you consider the otherwise billable time you and your staff expend in developing a proposal, you should feel that there is a potential for a return on your investment.

There are times when you should not expend much in the way of resources on preparing proposals. These include:

▲ When the request for the proposal is so specific about the requirements or definition of the type of firm sought that it is readily apparent that the contract has been "wired," i.e., the client already knows what firm he plans to hire and is merely going through the charade of seeking other bids.

▲ When the request is so generic that anyone and everyone has been invited to submit proposals. In such cases the client is usually going to base his decision on the basis of price, and the "winning" firm may easily wind up in a no-win situation.

▲ When it becomes apparent that the client really is not planning on hiring a consultant at all, and wants to simply gather ideas and suggested approaches from the proposals submitted so he/she can apply the techniques to solve the problem using his/her in-house staff.

▲ When the client does not have a specific problem that he wants help in solving at the present time and is asking for proposals to "keep on file" should the need arise.

In general, a proposal should be submitted only when you have some competitive advantage that enhances your chances of being selected for the assignment. Submitting proposals without some face-to-face selling in advance is risky and not very effective.

When you do decide to submit a proposal, be prepared to expend the resources necessary to insure that you do a good job and cover all the bases. A half-hearted effort is a wasted effort. A good proposal by itself probably won't be sufficient to land a contract, but a bad proposal will in all likelihood cause you to lose the assignment.

PROPOSAL WRITING

While each consulting firm may have its own format or style in preparing written proposals, there are some commonalities worth noting. For example, there is usually an opening section in which the consultant states his understanding of the issues or problems faced by the client. It helps the client to know specifically what the consultant does and does not plan to address during the project, and lets the client see if the consultant really understands his needs.

The next section typically states what the consultant proposes to do and outlines the projected results of his work, including the expected deliverables. This section also identifies how or in what form the results will be delivered to the client.

The consultant then explains in some detail the specific steps he/she plans to take to do the work. Depending upon how well you know and trust the client, you may want to leave a little bit of ambiguity as to exactly how you plan to proceed, lest it become a blueprint for the client (or one of your competitors) to follow and accomplish the task without you. You need to provide enough detail that it is apparent that you can do the job, but not enough that someone else can use your knowledge and not need your assistance.

Scheduling and responsibilities are the thrust of the next part of the proposal. The timing for conducting and completing the various phases of the project is outlined, and the names and pertinent information about the consultants who will be assigned to the engagement are included. This section or a separate section should include a statement about confidentiality and the ownership rights to any reports or findings.

The next section sets forth the cost to the client for the project and the basis on which the consultant priced the job, and should specify expense reimbursement expectations and billing and payment schedules.

The final part of the proposal should outline the benefits or results the client can expect from the project. Most successful consultants are able to help the client perceive the consulting engagement as an "investment" rather than a cost or expense.

Depending on the nature and scope of the engagement, proposals can be as little as a few pages written almost as a letter, or a bound document of a hundred pages or more, complete with charts, graphs, exhibits, and the like. Regardless of the length, it must be error-free and attractively laid out. After all, it is a statement about the adherence to quality and level of professionalism of your firm.

After submitting your proposal, follow up in a week or so by telephone to ask if the client received it, if there are any questions, and when a decision might be made. Before you call, however, prepare yourself by anticipating the client's questions. You don't want to be caught off guard, so make sure you have a copy of the proposal right in front of you before you place the call.

Handshakes and oral agreements are nice, and they convey a sense of trust, but they should not take the place of written contracts or proposals. Oral agreements are subject to memory lapses and different interpretations and distortions, especially if one or both parties are disappointed in the performance of the other party. Consulting is a profession, but it is also a business.

PRICING CONSULTING ENGAGEMENTS

The place to begin in establishing your fees and pricing proposals is by knowing your costs. There is no crystal ball or actuarial chart that can tell you what to charge for your services. There is no rule of thumb that says a compensation study should cost $X, or a manufacturing process project is worth $Y, or an IT implementation can command $Z.

Proposals and fees reflect what they will actually cost the consulting firm, plus a reasonable profit. That's the secret to pricing in a nutshell. The keys are knowing your costs and confining your costs and your services to the limits of the proposal. It's one thing to exceed the client's expectations, but quite another to give away your time by undertaking work outside the scope of the assignment. For example, if you agreed to conduct a training program, but the contract does not call for you to develop written reports, don't do it, or your costs can easily exceed the price you agreed to do the work for.

DETERMINING YOUR COSTS

The costs on which your pricing will be based must take into account a number of elements, such as:

1. The salary or income the consultants expect to receive annually.

2. The time actually available for consulting (take into account vacation time, holidays/weekends, travel time, nonbillable time, such as time for paperwork, marketing, continuing education, etc.).

3. Personal expenses (that are not reimbursable by a client) such as benefits, income, payroll and social security taxes, pension plans, insurance premiums, etc.

4. Overhead expenses such as rent, administration, telephones, etc.

For consulting firms, according to ACME's 1996 Survey of Key Management Information, on average employees worked 27–32 billable hours per week, and 95% of these billable hours were actually collected from clients. An average standard billing rate per hour was approximately $250 for Senior Partners, $200 for Junior Partners, and $163 for Senior Consultants.

Problem-Solver 4-7
ESTABLISHING AN HOURLY RATE

The Issue

How do I go about establishing an hourly rate to charge for my services?

Let's Work This Through

Let's say you are a one-person consulting firm, with an office and one support person, and you want to earn $75,000 per year in income before taxes. In theory, you have 2,080 hours available to work per year (40 hours × 52 weeks), so if you took no time off and worked every hour available, your hourly rate would be $75,000 ÷ 2080, or $36.05/hour.

But let's take out four weeks for vacation and sick days, and four weeks per year on paperwork, seminars, trade shows, etc. You're now down to 44 weeks, or 1,760 hours. Next, you'll have to devote at least 25% of your time to marketing activities, leaving your available time at 1,320 hours and increasing your billing rate to $56.82 ($75,000 ÷ 1320).

Now we need to add your personal benefits (insurance, pension, etc.) which generally run about 35% of salary. So you have to earn $101,250, not $75,000, and your rate has to be $101,250 ÷ 1320, or $76.70 per hour.

On top of this, we include office expenses of let's say $25,000 in salary + 30% benefits = $32,500, plus $1,000 a month rent and another $1,000 for utilities and supplies, for a total of another $56,500, bringing your hourly rate to $119.51 ($157,750 ÷ 1320).

We also need to add, profit before taxes, say 15% so you have something to reinvest in your firm for future growth and development, for an hourly rate of $137.44, or a daily rate of $1,100 to meet your financial goals.

ESTIMATING TIME

Determining your costs is actually the easy part of pricing a proposal. The hard part is estimating how long it will take you to complete the project in terms of person-days.

The key is to break down the engagement into phases such as literature review, interviews, report writing, etc. Then assign a realistic number of hours or days to complete each phase. Multiply the time by the daily or hourly rate of each consultant working on that phase, and add the amounts to arrive at an overall cost for professional fees. When calculating pricing, don't forget to add in the firm's targeted pre-tax profit margin if you didn't include it in calculating the daily or hourly rates of your consultants.

Time is especially difficult to calculate for consulting assignments because you are often at the mercy of the availability and schedule of the client, and are subject to travel delays, "telephone tag," and other circumstances over which you have little or no control. Build in room for contingencies.

FEE BASIS

Just as there are different ways for coming up with the cost of an assignment to the consultant, there are different ways of quoting the price to the client. Some of the more common concepts include:

▲ Hourly rates or time and material where you bill the client for the actual number of hours worked plus the cost of materials and reimbursable expenses.

▲ Per diem rates which may make the hourly rate seem more acceptable and gets away from the worry about long or short days.

▲ Special rates are variable rates depending on such things as: a client's demand that the consulting firm's CEO or another highly compensated specialist devote more time to the project than the work would ordinarily call for.

▲ High risk assignments, either from physical risk in politically sensitive geographical areas or a risk to your firm's reputation, such as providing expert witness testimony.

▲ Fixed price or not-to-exceed price is easier for clients to budget for, but requires the consultant to estimate carefully.

▲ Contingent fees where the consultant is "rewarded" based on the success of the engagement.

▲ A retainer is basically a payment for being available to the client for a certain amount of time per month.

▲ Product or per person rates can work for certain assignments such as surveys or training.

When considering pricing issues, it bears repeating that you should help the client to view the assignment as an investment in his company's future rather than as an expense. It also bears remembering that the perception of price is based on feelings, not on dollars and cents. When the client feels he received good value and service, the money is practically irrelevant to the client. And if you're in the consulting profession for the right reasons, money cannot be your prime motivator either.

5
PERFORMING AND MANAGING ENGAGEMENTS

WHERE THE RUBBER MEETS THE ROAD

Performing and managing engagements is where the rubber meets the road in consulting—the point at which the consultant applies his or her skills to the client's problem.

Regardless of the type of consulting, technical or process, or specific area of focus, strategy, marketing, productivity improvement, etc., while they are distinct in many ways, they all have certain elements in common:

▲ The objective of any consulting assignment is to help the client deal with change, either to manage it or to initiate it.

▲ The selling of the service and the providing of the service cannot be separated, because the selling of the service continues throughout the life of the project. The consultant must constantly reassure the client that the proper approach is being used, the right team is working on the project, and that recommendations being made will help bring about the desired results.

▲ The client's willingness to accept and implement the consultant's recommendations is directly influenced by how well the client perceives the management of the project.

At its most simplistic, managing a consulting engagement is the effective juggling of *Quality, Time,* and *Budget.* The client must feel the project was successful and you, the consultant, likewise should feel justifiably proud to attach your name to the finished product. The client wants his problem solved in a timely manner at a reasonable cost.

Problem-Solver 5-1

MANAGING TIME

The Issue

There simply aren't enough hours in the day. What can I do?

Let's Work This Through

Successful consultants are busy people. They have to find time to work on projects, meet with clients, market their services, be present for their family and find opportunities for personal and technical growth. In other words, consultants must be good at managing time.

The management of time is a state of mind. It requires shedding a lot of old habits in favor of Planning, Choosing, and Prioritizing. There are five major principles of time management:

1. There is no such thing as a lack of time to do the things you *want* or *need* to do.

2. Direct yourself toward effectiveness, not efficiency.

3. Time management takes will power and self-control.

4. Time management allows you to gain freedom and greater flexibility by taking back control of your life.

5. Ask yourself, "What is the best possible use of my time at this moment?"

As consultant, you want to make a reasonable profit and to have enough time to be able to gather the necessary data on which to base your recommendations. The most successful projects are those where the client and the consultant recognize and accept each other's needs and work together to insure that they both win.

LOOK BEFORE YOU LEAP

Once a consultant gets a client and a contract is signed, it is tempting to rush head-long into the assignment. This "damn the torpedoes, full speed ahead" approach is a recipe for failure, and contributes to much of the anti-consultant folklore. Bringing in an outsider is always perceived as a threat. False rumors as to why the consultant is there are bound to spread, especially among the client's employees who have never met or seen the interlopers/consultants. Many consultants who may have done a good job of solving problems have had their assignments sabotaged by ignoring the internal politics of the client organization.

The successful consultant carefully arranges to be introduced to the client organization. This begins by sitting down at the outset to go over the areas of sensitivity surrounding the assignment. It is important to have a clear understanding along a number of fronts, such as:

▲ Who will be your "champion" or "sponsor" within the client organization. Usually it will be the person who brought the consultant in who will be the primary contact, but it is wise to arrange to have other key executives in your corner to help you on a daily basis when the primary sponsor may be traveling. Having other people on your side also avoids the perception that you are the president's (or other executive that hired you) consultant, and instead makes you the organization's consultant.

▲ How you will be introduced to the client organization. This should be done in writing to forestall rumors and miscommunications. The notification of your involvement and request for assistance on the part of key executives should be signed by a high-level influential executive of the client organization. The letter of introduction should be sent to all key executives who will be affected by the project so they can learn about it officially and not through the grapevine. The notice should be honest about the focus of the assignment, the importance of employee cooperation, and an assurance that the consultant will treat employee comments as confidential. The presence of an "outsider" is always stressful to employees of the client organization. A proper introduction can help relieve some of their apprehension. But remember, a letter or notice of introduction, regardless of how carefully crafted, is not enough. You will have to introduce yourself over and over again as you travel about the organization. Don't assume everyone knows you or has read the memo. It is important for them to meet and hear from you directly to help them feel that they know about you.

▲ What kind of administrative support you will receive from the client organization, and who will coordinate this support. For example, if you need access to certain files, who will get them for you? Will you have the use of an office, and who will provide secretarial services if they are needed? Who will answer your telephone, etc.?

▲ What really is the political situation in that client organization? Find out where the land mines and quicksand pits are, and get an assessment of the level of support the consulting project actually has throughout the organization.

GET TO KNOW WHO'S WHO

In addition to sitting down and planning how you will be introduced into the client organization, it is crucial before the project gets underway for you to meet with the key influencers. These are the real "movers and shakers," who, regardless of their titles or position on the organization chart, can have a profound impact on the success of the consulting project. They can help you immeasurably, or convincingly sabotage the engagement. At the outset of any consulting assignment there will be some executive and staff members who will be disposed to favor the project, some will be anywhere from slightly to vehemently opposed, and the majority will take a wait and see attitude. While it may be tempting to side with those in favor of the project, it could be a fatal flaw to do so. Successful consultants carefully cultivate their objectivity and independence and are respected for doing so.

Meet with all of the key executives who are even remotely likely to be involved with or impacted by the consulting project. Become acquainted with the formal and informal organization hierarchies and reporting relationships. Remember, it is only human nature for the client staff to at least somewhat distrust you. They want to know who you are and why you're there. Your credibility and the success of the engagement can depend on how well you are able to answer these questions. At its heart, consulting is about relationships, not projects. By taking the time to get to know the client staff, you may actually save time over the long term, and will certainly enhance the chances of success of the project.

It may sound obvious, but it is extremely important to remember that every client is unique. Every client will have its own distinctive culture, mores, and internal politics. Successful consultants learn the nuances of each client and pay attention to the fact that any client organization is, at its core, a group of people. And like all groups of people, they will have ways of interacting that the consultant must pay attention to. Some of these cultural implications include how the client staff members address each other – by first or last name, how formally or informally they dress, who has the authority to make decisions, and what is the process by which the decisions are made. The more you can fit in with the client's culture rather than sticking out like a sore thumb, the better your chances of success.

REASSESSING THE PROBLEM

Clients hire consultants to help them solve a problem. However, the client may not be certain of what the exact problem is. Many times a client will know that something is wrong, but because they are so close to the situation they may not be able to see the whole picture. Or they develop a Request For Proposal (RFP) based on their

Problem-Solver 5-2
WINNING FRIENDS

The Issue

What can I do to increase my chances of being accepted by the client's employees?

Let's Work This Through

Several years ago Dale Carnegie wrote the book *How to Win Friends and Influence People* (©1936 by Dale Carnegie, published by the Pocket Books Division of Simon & Schuster, N.Y.) in which he outlined several techniques. Among the most compelling are:

1. Remember and use people's names when talking to them.

2. Encourage others to talk, and really listen to them before asking them to listen to you.

3. Praise other people when you can do it sincerely.

4. Don't argue, instead discuss issues without implying that anyone who disagrees with you is wrong.

5. Allow people to save face; if someone blunders, focus on solutions, not the mistake.

6. Ask questions or make requests rather than giving orders.

7. Praise even small achievements; encouragement is the best motivator.

8. Give the person a good image of himself to live up to; change behavior by raising self-esteem.

9. Make the other person feel happy about doing what you need done.

10. Get the other person in the mood to say yes before you ask the big question by establishing a pattern of favorable responses.

perceptions. As a consultant, you respond to the information contained in the RFP. But what if that information was wrong? It would be better to find out early on that you were brought in to solve the wrong problem, rather than waiting until the project is well under way and heading in the wrong direction.

Talk to several of the key executives you have had a chance to meet, and ask for their assessment as to what the problem really is and how well they think it was defined in the RFP and in your proposal. They may each have their own definition, so you will need to look for commonalities, or determine if there are big discrepancies as to where they see the problem emanating and how it can best be described. You can also ask how important they perceive the solving of the problem to be in comparison with other issues confronting the organization. If the problem you have been called in to work on is not seen as being sufficiently important, you may find it hard to solicit the input and participation you will need from the client staff. It is also a good idea to be on the lookout for any materials the executives might mention in passing that might have a bearing on your project. Who knows, maybe another consultant or staff team may have previously addressed the same problem and done some of your work for you.

Should you find a wide divergence in the definition of the problem or experience a lack of interest in solving it, you will need to go back to the client. Working together, you will hopefully be able to redefine the problem, refocus the project, identify ways to stimulate interest, etc. Remember, both you and the client want the consulting project to be successful. That won't happen unless you get off on the right foot (and, of course, solve the right problem).

ENGAGEMENT STRATEGY

To some extent the strategy you will use to conduct the engagement is determined by the objectives and requirements of the client. For example, the client may have his own deadline for completion of the project, which may be shorter than the consultant

---

Problem-Solver 5-3
TO DO LISTS

The Issue

I've got so much to do. How can I keep track of it all?

Let's Work This Through

Perhaps a "to-do" list can help you keep on top of what needs to get done. Here are some tips for making your list more manageable:

1. Prepare your list for tomorrow at the end of today.

2. Don't include routine items on your list.

3. List and identify all items that need special attention.

4. Rank the items on your list at A, B, or C in terms of priority, importance and effective use of your time.

5. Look for items you can delegate and delegate them.

6. Do the A items first, and get comfortable with not doing the C's.

7. At the beginning of each day, refer to your list.

would have preferred. This may cause you to adopt a different schedule than you would normally suggest. It is important from the outset to put together a suggested plan of action and to discuss it with the client so his views and priorities can be included. As the project progresses, the strategy should be periodically reviewed by both sides so the plan can be revised if needed.

In designing the engagement strategy, the following factors must be considered:

- ▲ The starting points of the assignment—not only the date on which the project will actually begin, but the actual physical location(s) where the consultant and client agree the project should begin.

- ▲ The pace of the work—how quickly the work is to be done in light of any deadlines, as well as how readily the client organization can assimilate change.

- ▲ The sequence in which problems are to be tackled and reports are to be made—you and the client need to know if the problem you have been hired to address cannot be solved without first addressing other issues, and the order in which they should be approached.

- ▲ When, how, and to whom interim reports and final recommendations are to be presented.

- ▲ When (or if) and how the consultant will assist in implementing the recommendations.

- ▲ The size and makeup of the consulting team and who will be the primary points of contact between the consultant and client.

- ▲ The number and profile of the people the client organization will assign to work with the consultants, and their level of expected participation on the project team.

STAFFING THE ENGAGEMENT

If you are a sole practitioner and the assignment calls for only one consultant, the decision as to who will staff the assignment is fairly easy. However, if the engagement calls for the involvement of more than one consultant, then some decisions need to be made. The desires and needs of the client must be balanced against the possibilities and interests of the consulting firm.

Obviously, every client wants the best and most experienced consultants to work on his project. Chances are that most of the consultants the client has met thus far were senior people, those who sold the assignment and negotiated the contract. He/she will undoubtedly expect the consultants assigned to his/her project to be of this same caliber. The consulting firm, on the other hand, would prefer to staff the engagement with lower level people for two very important reasons—lower level personnel need the experience, and the consulting firm's profits are, to a large part, contingent on the firm's ability to leverage its senior staff. This means using very few senior (and therefore more highly compensated) consultants to manage the project, with the work actually being performed by newer or lower level consultants. The consulting firm must be careful to avoid having the client think he was the victim of a "bait-and-switch" scheme where he thought he would be working only with senior people, but only junior consultants show up. Communication with the client is the key to avoiding misunderstandings.

Problem-Solver 5-4
COMMUNICATIONS AND LEADERSHIP

The Issue

I'd like to be a better leader for my staff and my clients. What do I need to do?

Let's Work This Through

Leaders help other people to achieve all that they are capable of; they establish a vision for the future; they encourage, coach, and mentor; and they establish and maintain successful relationships. Communication in turn is built on trusting relationships.

To make communication work:

1. Make communication a top priority.

2. Be open to other people.

3. Create a receptive environment for new ideas.

Communication is a two-way street. All the brilliant ideas in the world are wasted if you don't share them. Communication makes achievement possible.

The notion of "chemistry" or the correct matching of client and consultant personalities can make the difference between successful projects and failures. The consultant who sold the project should take notes as to the client's habits, likes and dislikes, and general characteristics. These attributes must be taken into account when selecting the consulting staff to assign. This is not to say that the client and consultant must necessarily have to have everything in common. In fact, sometimes it is necessary to assign a consultant of a very different type from the client on certain projects where a modifying influence is needed. The main thing is to avoid putting completely incompatibles together.

Before establishing assignment plans, the consulting firm needs to make sure that the consultants they want to work on the project will be available when needed and for the length of time needed.

This is another balancing act in which the consulting firm must be engaged. The firm wants to use the best consultants possible, but must also provide opportunities for growth and experience for all of its consultants. In addition, there may well be other projects going on at the same time where the same consultant is required. The successful consulting firm pays close attention to how and when projects are scheduled, and maintains an up-to-date database of the projects each of its consultants are working on. In addition, careful records are kept of each consultant's skills and experiences to ensure they can be assigned properly.

THE ENGAGEMENT PLAN

Successful consulting projects are the result of careful planning. The engagement plan should include a number of components in addition to time lines and staffing considerations. These include:

▲ Announcing the engagement—making sure that the highest ranking individual in the client organization you can get to do so writes and distributes an announcement that a consultant has been engaged, the reasons for doing so, and encouraging the client staff to be of assistance to the consultant as needed.

▲ The work plan—including tasks that need to be done and by whom, objectives and outputs at different stages of the engagement, staffing decisions, budget information, and a time line for completion and for intermediate steps.

▲ Requests for readily available data—a form letter request and check-off list of data you need from the client, such as: existing plans, financial statements, annual reports, 10-Ks, organization charts, etc.

▲ Data collection instruments you will need to design to gather information specific to the project for which you have been engaged.

▲ A sense or vision of what the deliverables will look like at the completion of the engagement.

▲ An understanding of how the client (and the consultant) defines "success" for the project.

Some final control steps before actually starting the project include:

▲ Confirming and clarifying the focus of the engagement and the scope of the plan with the client.

▲ Testing and validating the data collection instruments you plan to use by trying them out on a few members of the client staff before distributing them widely.

▲ Making sure the consulting staff clearly understands and will work within the time and budget constraints.

▲ Developing agreement as to expected quality of the content of reports and final product.

DATA COLLECTION

You are now ready to engage in the first phase of working on a project. While there is a wide range of situations that may differ somewhat depending on the nature of the particular assignment, there tends to be a common sequence of steps the consultant takes. Assuming the planning phase was handled properly and the scope of the project has been defined, the engagement will normally pass through the following four steps:

1. Data collection and fact finding.

2. Analysis of facts and information.

3. Recommendations.

4. Implementation.

While there will often be some overlapping of time and content among the four steps, successful project control involves the monitoring of progress step-by-step. The time and resources devoted to each step must be kept in proportion to the overall time and budget of the project.

An essential aim in following this four-step process is to achieve increasing accuracy in identifying and solving the real problem facing the client. Consultants are hired to recommend solutions, but the viability and usefulness of the recommendation will depend on how well the consultant understands the problem. As in the medical field, a wrong diagnosis will lead to an ineffective cure.

A second reason for following the four stages is that it helps to restrain the consultant's proclivity to make premature judgments as to the causes of the problem and the desire to offer solutions too early in the engagement. Remember, it is not unusual for the client to have misidentified the actual problem. It is even possible that the problem may have changed somewhat between the time the proposal was submitted and when work on the project begins.

Because problem identification is so crucial to project success, the consultant must avoid a number of pitfalls. The successful consultant:

▲ Will not simply accept the preliminary definition of the problem, but will undertake his/her own further diagnosis.

▲ Is prepared to re-examine and redefine the problem at any point in the assignment, even if it means revising his strategy and plan.

▲ Has a sense of proportion and priority to be able to recognize the difference between problems that require his and the client's attention and those that can be ignored or are cheaper for the client to live with than to solve.

▲ Realizes that large complex problems can be broken down into smaller problems which can be solved more easily.

▲ Will not try to solve every problem brought to his attention, especially those which are clearly beyond the scope of the consulting assignment.

Consultants gather data for a variety of reasons, the most obvious being to shed light on the client's problem. Data collection enables the consultant to differentiate between symptoms and the problem. Gathering data also often permits the consultant to uncover solutions to the problem which reside within the client organization. Even if the solution is not forthcoming from the data collected, the process of gathering information may help the consultant to identify the types of solutions which the client may find acceptable. Data also provides objective evidence to back up the consultant's recommendations and to lend credence to his/her conclusions. Yet another purpose of data gathering is to help keep the consultant from falling back on "pat" answers and recommendations. Even (maybe especially) experienced consultants have a set of theories and solutions which have served them well on other assignments, so there is a tendency to want to apply them to all clients. Proper data collection techniques restrain this desire and encourage objectivity.

Sound consulting work is built on facts. Facts are needed to get a clear picture of the situation, to accurately identify the problem, and to make sure recommendations are

Problem-Solver 5-5
WHY CLIENTS DON'T GIVE YOU THE FACTS

The Issue

The client and I both know that getting information is important, so why is it so difficult to get them to tell me what I need to know?

Let's Work This Through

Collecting and interpreting the right data and information is crucial to the success of a consulting project. Much of that information can be gathered directly from client personnel, but chances are they won't freely volunteer what they know for a variety of reasons, such as:

▲ The client and his/her employees are busy and don't have the time to tell you everything you'd like to know.

▲ Telling you the full story could be embarrassing to the client because he/she doesn't want you to know how little he/she may actually know about the issue or situation you have been called in to address.

▲ Some employees of the client organization are likely to feel that talking to you could hurt them, especially if they have negative comments about the company.

▲ Sometimes the clients don't want to "hang dirty laundry in public," so they attempt to cover up or gloss over internal squabbles.

▲ The client really doesn't understand what information you need or are looking for.

It is up to you as the consultant to help the client overcome these blocks to sharing the information you need to do your job.

---

based on reality. However, facts may be difficult to obtain, and gathering facts is often the most tiring phase of a consultant's work, but there is no alternative.

The kind of facts needed depends on the nature of the consulting engagement. It is also worth bearing in mind that seemingly identical types of data may have different meanings in different client organizations. For example, phrases like "work in progress" may be defined in a number of ways. Quantities may be subjected to rounding or different margins of error. The degree of detail of the facts required may differ for each project, as can the depth to which the consultant is expected (or is willing or able) to dig to unearth the facts. By and large, facts are available to the consultant in three forms:

▲ Records

▲ Actions and events

▲ Memories and perceptions

Any of these sources may be available within the client organization and/or from external materials such as publications, reports, and opinions of people outside the organization.

Records are facts stored in readable form. They include documents, files, films, tapes, charts, drawings, etc. The facts are obtained by retrieval, study, and analysis.

Actions and events and the circumstances surrounding them provide facts which can be observed and recorded.

Memories and perceptions are stored in the minds of people, and they represent facts which can be obtained by means of interviews, questionnaires, surveys, reports, etc.

The consultant and client should collaborate in deciding the sources of data to be used, how the data can best be collected, and who (consultant's staff, client staff, joint efforts) will participate in the collection of the data. Successful consultants will avoid indirect and time-consuming methods of collecting data if the same information can be obtained simply and directly. In effect, there are four primary data-collection techniques:

1. Interviews

2. Surveys

3. Observations

4. Document Analysis

Interviews are useful in all types of consulting assignments and are a primary source of a consultant's findings. In addition to providing a basis for information, they help to introduce and familiarize the consultant with the client's staff. Because they provide information about perceptions, feelings, memories, and opinions, interviews provide a richness and depth of data that cannot be obtained by any other means. However, there are also limitations and disadvantages to interviews. They rely on individual perceptions which are subject to distortion, either consciously or unconsciously, so the consultant would be well advised to double-check the opinions expressed either through additional interviews or by other data-gathering techniques. Interviews are also time-consuming and must be scheduled wisely, not only to avoid wasting time, but also to arrange for a representative sample of individuals from different levels and different groups or departments within the client organization. The consultant must also recognize that interviews require him to be a listener, and an objective listener at that, so as to avoid influencing the interviewee and biasing the results. Finally, two additional caveats concerning interviews are worth recalling—open-ended or carelessly worded questions may elicit opinions rather than facts, and confidentiality must be assured and maintained if you expect to get honest answers to your questions.

Problem-Solver 5-6
GETTING PEOPLE TO TALK TO YOU

The Issue

How do I get people to share with me the information I need?

Let's Work This Through

You need information to successfully complete the consulting assignment, but those who have the information you need will not talk freely. All human beings need encouragement to lower their inhibitions. Some ways of doing so include:

▲ Using positive feedback to let the person know how helpful they can be or have been.

▲ Letting the person know that you realize talking to you and sharing information is difficult for them, and that you understand and appreciate their predicament.

▲ Assisting, the client to understand how giving you the information will actually help him, since the project will benefit his company.

▲ Being open, friendly, and easy to talk to. Be the kind of person people want to talk to.

▲ Letting, people know that they can use you to "dump on" and get rid of pent-up feelings without being judged by you.

Surveys and questionnaires can be a powerful tool for gathering a great deal of information in an efficient manner. They can be used to solicit input from many more people than can be interviewed, and, in general, are more objective and elicit numerical values which are helpful in analysis. Disadvantages of surveys are their high costs (for designing, printing, and analyzing) and their potential to derive superficial information if the questionnaires are not carefully designed and analyzed. Surveys require an assurance of confidentiality, and should be structured so that most questions can be answered quantitatively to facilitate tabulation and objectivity. They should also avoid questions which can be responded to with a simple "yes or no," and avoid scales which do not allow for clear differentiations. Two additional considerations concerning surveys involve the way the questionnaire is introduced (i.e., the level of support for the survey on the part of the client CEO and/or other high-level executives as evidenced by the style and tone of the cover letter the client uses to inform his organization about the survey) and the importance of conducting follow-up interviews to clarify ambiguous results.

Observations are measurements of actual events rather than a collection of perceptions. By watching unobtrusively, the consultant can see what is really going on and can compare the reality to the responses received from interviews and surveys. However, acute observation skills are difficult to learn, and quite often the consultant is so busy or absorbed in the project that he misses significant events occurring right before his eyes. The consultant must also learn to differentiate between what is being *said* and what is being *done*. Words and behaviors may often differ, such as when teamwork and participation are talked about, but decisions are made autocratically. It is helpful, therefore, for the consultant to be attuned to nonverbal cues about the client culture. Do people smile and act friendly? Do they gather together and chat or sit behind their own closed office doors? How do they dress, how formal are they when addressing each other, etc.? Nonverbal behaviors often speak volumes.

Document Analysis is too often neglected by consultants as a very valuable source of information. In fact, quite often at least a partial solution to the client's problem is already available within the client organization before the consultant is brought in. For some reason consultants seem to feel that they must always develop their own data—even if it means re-inventing the wheel. The wise consultant will take the time to review client files pertaining to his project. He/she will also read the company's financial statements and annual reports, and will even conduct a literature search to see if any articles about the client have appeared in general business or trade publications. Other types of information worth reviewing include organization charts, performance appraisals, employee turnover and absentee reports, etc. As the consultant, the better forewarned and armed you are with available data before beginning in-depth data collection, the better off you will be. At the very least, it may prevent you from asking embarrassing questions and looking silly when the answer has already been made public.

FACT ANALYSIS

The second major phase of most consulting assignments consists of analyzing the facts which have been gathered during the data-collection step. Quite often so much data has been collected that the consultant can feel overwhelmed by the sheer volume and perceived complexity. The key is to keep the objective of the engagement in mind and to focus your analysis of the facts with this in mind. It also helps to remember that the ultimate aim of the assignment is to bring about change, and the analysis of the facts should help you determine:

▲ Whether change is necessary.

▲ Whether change is possible.

▲ What change is possible.

▲ What alternatives or recommendations are likely to be most effective.

Making sense out of all the data available usually begins with establishing the criteria by which the data is to be organized and tabulated. The most common classifications used in management consulting projects are by:

▲ Time, which indicates trends, rates of change, fluctuations.

▲ Place or unit within the organization.

▲ Responsibility for facts and events.

▲ Structure which shows how changes in components affect the whole entity.

▲ Influencing factors that appear to cause changes.

The purpose of the analysis is to identify:

▲ The *nature* of the problem to be solved.

▲ The *cause* of the problem.

▲ The *impact or implications* of the problem.

▲ The *relationships* between factors.

In a nutshell, fact analysis starts the process of developing recommendations and identifies the factors and elements that have to be changed if the client's problem is to be solved and the assignment is to be successful.

DEVELOPING RECOMMENDATIONS

When the analysis of facts has been completed and some conclusions drawn, the consulting assignment enters its principal stage—the development, evaluation, and presentation of proposed recommendations.

In most cases, the client has brought a consultant in with the expectation that the consultant will find and recommend the best solution to the client's problem. However, there are often reasons for identifying alternatives. In the first place, most management problems do not have only one solution; they can be solved in several different ways. The client may be more comfortable that the consultant has reviewed the problem from different sides and wants to be presented with alternative solutions before making up his/her mind.

The consultant draws from a variety of sources in putting together alternative recommendations including:

▲ His/her own prior experience and previous assignments.

▲ Files and documentation the consulting firm may have from other projects.

▲ Input from colleagues in the consulting firm or in the consultant's network who have worked on similar projects.

▲ Professional literature.

▲ Input and recommendations from staff members in the client company.

The ability to relate things or ideas which were previously unrelated is one of the greatest attributes of successful consultants; it is also a definition of *creative thinking*. There are five stages in the creative thinking process. They require practice, but are well worth learning.

1. Preparation—Getting the facts, analyzing the data, defining the problem in different ways.

2. Effort—Divergent thinking about the problem and alternative solutions.

3. Incubation—Allowing the problem to percolate in the subconscious mind while moving on to other things.

4. Insight—A sudden flash or intuition that gives an answer and leads to possible solutions.

5. Evaluation—Analyzing all the ideas obtained.

The purpose of evaluating alternative recommendations is to provide an objective basis for choice. The client usually expects the consultant to prepare an evaluation of the various alternatives available. The consultant is also expected to suggest the alternative he/she would choose if he/she were in the client's shoes.

In presenting his/her suggestions, the consultant should state them in terms of:

▲ Findings of the data collection phase.

▲ Advantages of the recommended approach.

▲ Requirements and resources needed.

▲ Relationships to other proposals.

In most assignments the client is going to "test" the findings and recommendations against certain criteria, including:

▲ Are the findings supported by the facts?

▲ Are the findings "important?"

▲ Do the findings respond to the engagement criteria?

▲ Do the recommendations respond to the criteria?

▲ Do the findings support the notions of a "successful" project?

▲ Is the plan of action realistic?

The consultant must rely on more than hunches or a few opinions gathered during the interview process. Throughout the consulting process, the consultant must constantly be aware that there are a number of factors which can lead to a failed project. Some of the more common sources of error include:

▲ Misdirection—solving the wrong problem.

▲ Sampling—data not representative of the organization as a whole.

▲ Data source bias—hidden agendas and outright sabotage.

▲ Interpretation—understand meanings, not just words or actions.

▲ Averages—statistics can be misleading.

▲ Selectivity—hearing only what you want to hear.

▲ Meaningless differences—not every relationship is cause- and -effect.

▲ Jumping to conclusions—developing the answer too early.

▲ Emotional appeal—"correctness" is not always correct.

▲ Status—playing up to the boss.

PRESENTATION OF RECOMMENDATIONS

The presentation of the project deliverables requires planning on the part of the consultant. The nature of the assignment and the working relationship between the consultant and client will determine when and how the presentation of results will be made.

In some assignments, the client's staff has been directly and intimately involved in the project and keeps senior management informed of progress throughout the engagement. The presentation of findings and recommendations, therefore, does not bring anything new. In effect, in these cases the presentation involves summarizing the efforts, confirming the findings, and allowing or facilitating the client to make a decision.

In other cases, the scope or nature of the project may not require reporting and discussions at each step. Other projects may be of such a confidential nature (e.g., reorganizations) that the client does not want to hold many meetings or have information floating around before solutions have been fully defined. In this case the recommendations will represent completely new information.

In planning the presentation, the consultant should bear in mind a number of points. The following might serve almost as a sort of checklist for the consultant to consider in structuring a presentation:

▲ *What Is The Objective?* Why are we making this presentation, and how much of it will be new information to the client? What do we want the client to <u>do</u> as a result of the recommendations?

▲ *What Are We "Delivering?"* Is it a single recommendation, or alternative courses of action? A final report, or a suggested implementation plan? Are we providing a turnkey system, or guidelines for purchases?

▲ *Who Is The Immediate Audience?* How many people and at what level in the client organization are they? Will the information we are providing them be new, or a restatement of what they already know? Will our "champion" or the person who hired us be in the audience?

▲ *Will There Be Other Audiences?* Will this be a one-time presentation or just one of a series? Where will the other presentations take place, and who will be in each audience? Will our client contact be present at each presentation?

▲ *What Is The Client's Style?* Does the client like high-tech presentations with lots of "glitz," or is he a "just the facts" kind of person? How formal or informal should the presentation be? How will our style of presenting be received?

▲ *What Questions Will We Be Asked?* Are we prepared for the tough questions? Do we have the data and facts available to back up our findings? Who will answer the questions?

▲ *What Questions Will We Ask?* Are there points not covered in our presentation that we would like to have addressed, such as implementation plans and our role in those plans, etc.? We should also ask if there is anything else we may be able to help this client with now that we have come to know each other.

The objective of the presentation is to get the client to accept the recommendations. If the presentation works through a logical series of steps and builds up the case for the recommendations properly, the client should have little hesitation in accepting them. At least that is what should happen. If you don't think the probability of acceptance is high, hold off on the presentation and talk to the client privately.

Do not try to dazzle the client with your technique or bury the client in details. Above all, be honest with the client, especially concerning the risks involved and the conditions the client must create or maintain for the recommendations to be fully effective.

Successful consulting is much more than presenting solutions; it also involves patient persuasion and explanation to the client. This in turn means that the consultant must be aware of the client's personal biases and preferences which affect his decision making process. This awareness helps the consultant to frame the proposals and presentation in a way that will facilitate acceptance.

Once the presentation(s) have been given by the consultant and a decision made by the client, the assignment may be over from the consultant's point of view if the client plans to implement the recommendations himself. However, if the client prefers further assistance from the consultant, the next phase of a consulting engagement begins.

IMPLEMENTATION

Implementation is the final step in management consulting assignments, and the basic purpose of the engagement from the client's point of view. Obviously, the consultant, too, wants his/her recommendations not only to be well received, but to be implemented with good results as well. In years gone by, however, most consulting assignments ended with the delivery of a report and recommendations by the consultant. Today, it is more often the case that the consultant will be expected to participate in the implementation of those recommendations.

As a rule, the consultant will participate in implementation in one or more of the following ways:

- ▲ By providing advice and guidance to the client staff responsible for implementing the required changes.

- ▲ By working out the details of the proposals made, including the establishment of time frames and helping the client to assign and monitor responsibilities and progress.

- ▲ By training the client staff.

Over time, the consultant will assume less and the client staff will take on more responsibility for the implementation and ongoing changes. The goal should be for the consultant to make himself expendable, and for the client to become self-sufficient.

Unfortunately, for most consultants, implementation is the weakest link of the consulting process. Too many consultants seem to have the mistaken notion that change will somehow automatically occur just because a report and list of recommendations have been delivered. Other consultants picture themselves as analyzers who view implementation as the purview of line managers, and as consultants they are somehow above "getting their hands dirty" on such things as implementation.

Yet it is implementation that makes the difference between successful consultants and mediocre consultants. The real value of a consulting engagement is found in providing actual solutions to client problems. Bringing about change is at the heart of successful consulting. In today's vernacular, as a consultant you must be able to "walk the talk."

FACILITATING CHANGE

Accomplishing change in a client organization involves a series of stages, the first of which calls for the client to recognize that change is necessary. An illustration of this point is found in the story of a person walking down the street who passes by the porch of a house where a man is sitting, and at his feet lies a dog that is whimpering. The person asks the man on the porch why his dog is crying, and the man replies, "I guess he's lying on a nail." "Well, why doesn't he move?" asks the walker, to which the man responds, "I guess it doesn't hurt badly enough." If the client is not sure that the problem is sufficiently "painful" to cause him to take action, change is unlikely to occur. It has been said that the only person who likes a change is a wet baby, so the consultant often needs to find a way to make the client accept the fact that change is necessary. Sometimes this is accomplished if the client is surprised by the findings contained in the final report and becomes motivated to take action. Other times it may mean the consultant has to confront the client with the necessity of change.

The next stage involves the client staff in actually beginning to make the changes called for. It is important that early successes be achieved, so the easiest steps should be scheduled to take place first. However, the consultant must not try to make the client move too far too quickly. Unrealistic demands serve no purpose. People can accept change and move only as fast as their attitudes and abilities will let them.

The final stage in the change process involves providing encouragement and reinforcement to the client staff as they begin to change. The reinforcement must come from both the consultant and the top management of the client organization. If the leadership of the client company is not overtly supportive of the changes in process, lower-level employees will have little reason to get on the bandwagon. The consultant can assist in this process by insuring that the client's senior executives participate in the program and are united behind the change initiatives. Lower-level employees will watch their superiors' actions, and lip service is not enough. As always, actions speak louder than words.

6
STAFFING ISSUES

RECRUITING AND RETAINING GOOD PEOPLE

"Management Consultants Are Enjoying A Boom," proclaimed the headline of the November 26, 1995 issue of the *National Business Employment Weekly* published by the *Wall Street Journal.* Quoting the author of this book, the article goes on to note that consulting firm CEOs say their top concern is not finding more business, but rather "finding and retaining good people."

Notwithstanding an increased need to add to their staffs, consulting firms are not "body shops" willing to hire any and all applicants. It is no longer sufficient to be "the best and the brightest" with a newly minted MBA degree from a prestigious institution of higher learning. The days of the generalist, if not over, are certainly waning. Clients are not willing to be on-the-job training centers for consultants. Today's clients expect consultants to provide specific industry experience or technical expertise. This has led to increased competition among consulting firms as they seek to hire, not only the best people seeking to enter the field, but also to recruit experienced consultants away from each other—a practice that only a few short years ago was thought to be unprofessional.

At its core, consulting is a people business. It doesn't matter if the nature of the engagement calls for the development of a strategic plan, the design and installation of a computer system, or the implementation of a new accounting process; the fundamental essence of consulting remains with human beings relating to human beings. No software program or computational model can replace a human consultant's ability to understand and empathize with the client's symptoms while still being able to comprehend the underlying problem, diagnose it properly, and develop creative solutions.

Consulting projects succeed or fail on the basis of the abilities of the people assigned to the project. If the client does not feel that the consultant was perceptive, sensitive to his needs, and/or was not able to communicate clearly, the client will not be convinced that his problem was solved. Fancy reports and turnkey systems will not take the place of the "chemistry" which must exist between the consultant and the client if the client is to feel that the consulting engagement was truly successful.

Therefore, consulting firms are justifiably "picky" when it comes to hiring new consultants, and they are willing to spend a considerable amount of money in an attempt to get the right people. The June 1996 issue of *Consultants News* estimates that major consulting firms spend an average of $90,000 on each new recruit.[1] What makes this number even more interesting is that it takes the firm about two years to break even on a new MBA recruit—and the average stay of a new MBA at their first consulting firm is only two to three years! No wonder consulting firms are so desirous to hire already experienced consultants away from one another.

Problem-Solver 6-1
PEOPLE PROBLEMS

The Issue

I just want to consult; how come I seem to spend so much time dealing with people problems?

Let's Work This Through

Once you expand beyond a sole practitioner consulting operation, spending time on people is what running a firm is all about.

▲ If it's growing quickly, you'll have to spend significant amounts of time on recruiting and training. Both are people issues.

▲ If it is growing more slowly, you'll need to spend time on enhancing the skills of your present staff and making sure your firm's strategic direction is properly focused. Again, these are people issues.

▲ Client relationship management, marketing, team formation and development, and all of the other myriad activities that go into running a firm are all people issues.

Spend time dealing with people and developing a dedicated staff and loyal client base, and your firm will succeed.

Based on my discussions with the directors of recruiting at several leading management consulting firms, there are certain common techniques they use and questions they ask when interviewing candidates for employment with their firms. Here's what they are looking for:

INTERVIEW CRITERIA (Looking for degree of preparation and introspection)

▲ Academic track record

▲ Intellectual skill

▲ Accomplishments

▲ Team building/interpersonal skills

▲ Communication skills (written/oral)

▲ Problem solving/analytic skills

▲ Technical skills (if required at entry level; such as computer knowledge, etc.)

▲ Relevant work experience

▲ Selling skill

▲ Work ethic

▲ Diversity of interests

▲ Motivational skills

▲ Corporate/work environment criteria (i.e., culture fit)

▲ Career criteria

THOUGHT PREPARATION. Avoid focusing your preparation on "what" type responses (resumes provide this information). Focus on "how/why" responses to these commonly asked interview questions. Here are some ideas of what the consulting firm will be looking for in your response to various questions:

One other thing to bear in mind if you are going to be interviewed for a position with a consulting firm is to attend the interview dressed like a consultant. This should go

Question	To Evaluate
Tell me about yourself.	Open-ended quick thinking, organization, reaction to a potentially unsettling question.
How did you choose your school/discipline?	Planning, decision making, maturity of thought.
What courses did you excel at/why?	Motivation, interests.
What courses interested you least/why? How did you do in these courses?	Adversity, achievement.
How did you spend your time outside the classroom?	Diversity, time management, motivation.
What was the most difficult situation you faced in school and how did you deal with it?	Adversity, problem solving.
What is the biggest disappointment you've faced in life so far, and how did you deal with it?	Adversity, problem solving.

continued

Question	To Evaluate
What do you consider your top 2–3 accomplishments in life? What was the personal satisfaction derived from these situations?	Motivation, achievement.
What's the most satisfying work experience(s) you've had and why?	Work ethic corporate culture fit, motivation, accomplishment, career interest.
What 2–3 qualities must exist in a work environment to stimulate you?	Corporate culture criteria.
What typically motivates you in your activities, be they work, school, or play?	Motivation, corporate culture fit.
Have you ever participated in a group or team activity? If yes, put yourself in the shoes of a team member and describe (name of interviewee) to me in terms of his/her participation style and contribution.	Interpersonal, team player.
What 2–3 qualities do you like least in others?	Interpersonal, corporate culture fit.
What qualities do you admire most in others?	Interpersonal, corporate culture fit.
What 1–2 qualities do you like least about yourself? How are you overcoming these?	Introspection, interpersonal developmental.
What's your criteria for selecting this career?	Thought preparation, career interest.
What's your criteria for selecting our company?	Thought preparation, career/corporate interest.
What kind of career objectives do you have for yourself over the next 3–5 years?	Goal setting, ambition, introspection.
Why should we consider hiring you?	Selling.

without saying, but I have participated as an interviewer on behalf of consulting firms far too many times where a candidate shows up dressed inappropriately. I can appreciate the fact that students may not have a lot of money to spend on business type clothing, but believe me, your investment will be well worth it. You don't get a second chance to make a first impression.

HIRING DO'S AND DON'TS

Find, attract, and hire the best person you can for each job for the money you can afford to pay. Hire people smarter than yourself—it's the firm's overall success that counts, not your ego.

There are some do's and don'ts that are worth considering when you set about hiring people for your firm. These include:

DO:

▲ Define the job as carefully and completely as you can so you will know what you want the new person to do.

▲ Define the capabilities the person will need to do the job.

▲ Encourage your present employees to recommend people they know for positions with your firm.

▲ Have more than one person interview the candidate.

▲ Conduct reference checks even if all the information you get is dates and places of employment and eligibility for being rehired.

▲ Describe the position as realistically as possible, both the good and the negative parts of the job, so the prospective employee will have realistic expectations.

▲ Be open about reporting relationships, both formal and informal, and be honest about growth and promotion opportunities.

▲ Write an offer letter to each person you decide you want to hire, spelling out the position, compensation arrangements, starting date, and the time frame for which the offer is valid.

There are also some traps that you can fall into during the hiring process. So pay attention to these:

DON'T:

▲ Hire someone unless they are the best possible candidate for the present position. Hiring for a potential position you hope to create or hoping that the candidate will grow into the present position is almost always a mistake.

▲ Rush the process. Take your time to properly interview candidates and to evaluate your thoughts about each of them before arriving at a decision.

▲ Think you have to do it alone. Hiring executive search consultants can often bring you better candidates than you might be able to identify on your own and can cut down on the number of interviews *you* have to conduct.

Hiring activities can seem to take a lot of time out of your busy schedule, but the long-term future of your firm is at stake. It is far wiser and more cost-effective to take the time to hire the right person each time than to have to re-do the process. Remember, every new hire will impact the profitability of your firm and, to a greater or lesser degree, will affect its culture as well. You can't afford not to do it right.

Problem-Solver 6-2
HIRING SENIOR-LEVEL PEOPLE

The Issue

Are there any tips for hiring senior-level people I should know?

Let's Work This Through

Proven performance is what counts, not credentials.

▲ Hire for track records of performance, not resumes.

▲ Look for consulting experience, not academic or general business experience.

▲ Trust your instincts regarding chemistry and culture fit.

▲ No matter how prestigious a firm they come from or how good their references are, interview them carefully.

TEN TRAITS OF SUCCESSFUL CONSULTANTS

Successful consultants possess a rather unique blend of skills and attributes. Too many people believe that because they have been successful business executives, they can easily make the transition and automatically become successful consultants. In reality, the skill sets are quite different, and for many people, not transferable. For example, executives are used to having the authority to have their decisions carried out; consultants make recommendations which may or may not be acted upon.

So, what are the skills required to be a good consultant? Management consultants themselves have been discussing these characteristics for years. The conclusion is the same as for any other profession that has attempted to develop an ideal candidate profile—there is no one and only one profile, but there are certain common characteristics which tend to correlate with success in consulting and the consultant's job satisfaction. In general, while many other occupations call for high levels of technical knowledge, management consulting requires a combination of technical competency, communications skills, and personal attributes. Based on my interviews with dozens of consulting firms and my own experience, the key characteristics may be summarized in the following ten traits:

1. *Integrity*—Consulting projects can affect the lives of many people, including employees, investors, and customers of the client organization. With vested interests at stake, these groups will seek to influence the consultant's thinking and the course of the recommendations. Thus, your integrity and adherence to ethical standards must remain scrupulous and avoid catering to the demands of any one group over another. Any diminishment of your integrity can harm others and yourself.

2. *Salesmanship*—The consultant who waits for clients to beat a path to his/her door will soon be out of business. Consultants must sell their services. In fact, successful consultants tend to devote approximately twenty-five percent of their time on marketing activities. It is very easy to fall into the trap of spending all of your time on the project at hand, only to come to realize that you have no work to do once that engagement has ended. Wise consultants try to schedule assignments to avoid this feast or famine cycle. Selling begins with the initial contact of the client, is crucial at the proposal stage, must be maintained throughout the assignment, is an integral part of presenting your recommendations, is necessary for obtaining additional assignments from the client at the conclusion of a project, and should continue even after your work for that client is finished. Since you are already familiar with the client organization, you may be able to identify new problems where you may be able to help in the future. Successful consultants maintain periodic scheduled contact with all of their former clients to keep their names on the minds of their clients.

3. *Diplomacy*—Consultants have little, if any, authority to make things happen. You must rely on your ability to persuade the client to take action. This is an area in which former business executives who try to become consultants often have a hard time making the transition from being a decision maker to being an influencer. Consulting also requires an ability to balance and often to mediate the often conflicting demands made by parties affected by the consulting project. The consultant is often caught in the middle of disputes between such factions as Labor vs. Management, Customer vs. Supplier, Production vs. Design vs. Marketing, etc. Since the consultant has the responsibility for the success of the project, but lacks the authority to make things happen, strong diplomatic skills are vital.

4. *Communication* skills—You may possess all nine of the other skills listed, but if you can't communicate effectively, your career in consulting will be very short-lived. Rapport and understanding between the consultant and client is the basis for the feeling of "chemistry" which must exist if the project is going to be truly successful from the client's point of view. And rapport and understanding are grounded in good communication without which you will not be able to sell a proposal, gather accurate data from interviews, or have your recommendations accepted. At the top of the list among communications skills needed by consultants is *sharp listening skills*. Being able to draw information out of a reluctant interviewee will greatly influence how a problem is perceived. Clients tend to judge consultants on their willingness to listen to them. It is an all too common mistake consultants make, trying to dazzle clients with the breadth of their knowledge by talking too much. An adage I often use with those seeking to enter the field of consulting is to "remember, we were created with two ears and one mouth—they should be used proportionately." *Cogent writing* ability is the means by which the consultant demonstrates that he has listened to and understands the needs of the client. If your proposal is not clear and to the point, or contains typos or misspelled words, your chances of winning a client are nil. If your final report is not succinct and cogent and your recommendations are not clear and concrete, there will be little chance of implementation. *Oral presentation skills* are necessary in making reports to the client. It is not enough to know the answers, you must be able to clearly respond to the questions that will inevitably arise during meetings. A single poorly phrased response can cast a shadow over your entire credibility. A poor performance during a presentation can cause the client to disregard your written report. And finally, a consultant needs a broad range of *intervention skills*. You must be able to guide the client back to the point of the interview when he begins to meander. Your ability to diffuse tension and resolve conflicts will be put to the test when the almost inevitable arguments break out among the client staff members and executive corps. When progress gets bogged down by details, you must be able to intervene to keep things moving.

5. *Flexibility*—No two clients are exactly the same; in fact, they may differ widely. Even if you consult within a particular industry, the culture of different client organizations will likely test your ability to adapt. Different dress codes, levels of formality and informality, decision-making processes, and personalities of the people you have to deal with will be different for each client. An ability to adapt and fit in is very helpful in gaining the trust of the client. A consultant that sticks out like a sore thumb does not engender openness on the part of the client staff. Flexibility and an ability to travel

are key components of the consulting lifestyle. Consulting is not a 9-to-5 and home-for-dinner-every-night type of life. Travel up to 60% or more of your time is not uncommon, long work days are the norm, and even weekends are often spent on the road.

6. *Diagnostic and problem-solving skills*—Consultants are problem finders as well as problem solvers. Rarely will the client accurately identify the problem at the outset of the project. More than likely you will have to ferret out the underlying causes. You must learn to be objective in assessing the opinions expressed by client staff and avoid taking sides so as to maintain a sense of independence. It also helps to be curious by nature and even being nosy is a positive attribute to help you avoid superficial or simplistic explanations. By and large, consultants are the type of people who enjoy puzzles and can find patterns running through diverse pieces of information. They can then conceptualize creative solutions to the client's problems based on their vision and insight. The most successful consultants have the additional ability to teach the client staff. For change to occur, and especially for change to last, clients must be trained to act differently than they had been acting.

7. *Self-discipline*—Without doubt, consultants are generally very bright people. Most have advanced degrees and enjoy being on the cutting edge of new developments in their chosen field of expertise. Yet it is the client who is the "boss," even if the client is not as well educated or as sophisticated as the consultant. It takes a good deal of self discipline to remember this. You must also discipline yourself to take care of yourself emotionally and physically. Travel, restaurant meals, receptions, late night meetings, client demands, and the stressful nature of the consulting business do not foster a healthy lifestyle. Without preventative self care, it is very easy for even otherwise highly successful consultants to burn out.

8. *Resourcefulness*—If solutions to client problems were readily available, the client would find the answer on his own. Clients expect consultants to be ahead of the curve when it comes to knowledge of their field of expertise, and to be able to locate and access hard-to-get reference materials. The client will expect you to be informed and articulate about the latest management techniques and theories, and your resourcefulness will be tested as you seek to develop innovative solutions based on a combination of theories supported by appropriate research findings. You may not know all of the answers to all of the questions, but you will be expected to be able to find (or develop) answers to most of them.

9. *Self confidence*—As a consultant, when things go wrong (and they will) during a project, you will be blamed; when things go right, the client takes the credit. If you need to have center stage and rely on the recognition of others to stroke your ego, consulting is not the field for you. Consultants derive satisfaction from knowing that they are good at what they do. And at times you may be called upon to defend the strength of your convictions by telling a client what he/she needs to hear even when he/she does not want to. But most of the time you will be working backstage, and even when the project is a huge success, it is unlikely that the client will say "thank you" or even acknowledge your contributions. Most good consultants are highly altruistic and enjoy knowing that they have helped their clients succeed, even if they do not get accolades for having done so. Successful consultants must be self-confident, self-motivated, self-fulfilled, and practitioners of the power of positive thinking. For consultants, every challenge is a new opportunity, and every failure represents a learning experience.

10. *Creative time management*—In addition to everything else, consultants must be able to juggle numerous, often conflicting, demands for their time and attention. It is rare that a consultant will be able to focus solely on only one client or one project for any considerable length of time. More often, assignments will overlap. And even if you are able to devote yourself to only one client or project, you must still find time to market. On top of this, you may have a family which expects some of your time. And then there is the need for continuing professional development, community or parental involvement programs, and if you can swing it, maybe even some time for socializing or personal growth. If ever bi-location were to become possible, I'm sure consultants would be the first users. Consultants learn to manage their time effectively; if they don't, they will soon be looking for another line of work.

ADDITIONAL TRAITS OF SUPERIOR CONSULTANTS

Truly successful consultants have learned to master the ten traits listed above. They also have developed another set of skills which enable them to rise to the top of their profession. These additional characteristics include:

1. *Relationship building*—The best consultants are those who can cultivate and manage relationships with their clients. They do everything they can to gain the trust and confidence of the client. Their focus is on the long-term relationship, not just the short-term project. They will walk the extra mile

to keep the client happy and to exceed the client's expectations. These are the people who will put extra time and effort into a project to ensure the client views it as a success, even if it means not billing the client for the additional time.

2. *Management ability and group dynamics skills*—Many people go into consulting to escape or avoid line management responsibilities. Yet as their firms grow and diversify, managerial tasks fall squarely on the shoulders of consultants. Those who can wear the mantle advance to leadership positions. I have often described running a consulting practice as being akin to trying to herd cats. Because they are bright, creative, self-confident, and able to work without direct supervision, consultants can be notoriously independent-minded. Yet teamwork is essential when a diverse group of talents is brought together to work on consulting assignments. Without skilled leadership, the project could soon turn into chaos. Successful engagements do not happen by accident. They are the result of good project management and group dynamics techniques. Likewise, successful consulting firms thrive because they are well managed. It takes a special kind of person to be both a good consultant and a good manager.

3. *Organizational awareness*—The best consultants are able to keep the big picture in sight. They can envision and help the client to understand the client organization as a system, and to see how a problem, or even the solution to a problem in one area, will impact other parts or departments of the company. They can see interrelationships and can avoid "the operation was a success, but the patient died" type of error. They are also very good at identifying additional areas of opportunity for their consulting firm to be of service to the client by helping the client to recognize other problems which need to be solved.

4. *Ability to develop others*—Training and mentoring new consultants are critical to a consulting firm's future. Yet far too few experienced consultants are willing to devote the time necessary to nurture and develop their successors. The true professionals in the consulting ranks recognize and accept their obligations and share their "secrets" with the next generation of consultants.

TRAINING OF CONSULTANTS

Where and how do consultants come by the skills necessary to succeed? Some of the attributes seem to be natural gifts which lend credence to those who would say that consultants are born, not made. There is some truth to this supposition, but even natural talents can be enhanced by training and experience.

First, there is formal education. Many consultants hold degrees from top graduate schools, and, for several firms, an MBA degree seems to be almost a prerequisite for consideration for employment. In today's highly competitive world, even a business degree must be augmented by a specialization in fields such as finance, marketing, or computer science.

Problem-Solver 6-3
KEEP YOUR PEOPLE HAPPY AND CONTROL EXPENSES

The Issue

I want to keep my employees happy, but I also have to keep expenses under control. What can I do?

Let's Work This Through

Consultants are bright people. They know you have a business to run, and most will be willing to work with you to control expenses, if you let them in on the reasons you need to, especially when times are good.

▲ Explain how you plan to use the profits to better the firm in the future by investing in R&D of new products and services.

▲ Show how investments in advertising, PR, and other marketing activities will benefit the firm and the employees through new business.

▲ Emphasize how the employees will share in profits, such as bonuses, profit sharing plans, 401(K) matching contributions, etc.

Your staff members want to be treated as "partners" in the firm's success, not simply as employees. Give them a real sense of participation, not just a paycheck.

In addition to a graduate degree, most consulting firms require candidates for employment to have had actual work experience. Many firms look for people who have a hands-on understanding of the workings of a particular industry, such as financial services. Other firms seek experience in a functional area like human resources. The theory one learns in school must be tempered by the hard knocks and lessons learned in an actual work setting.

Most large consulting firms provide their staff consultants with extensive training programs. These learning opportunities are designed to teach new hires the firm's consulting services and methodologies, as well as to provide seasoned veterans with an opportunity to upgrade their skills.

Finally, there is the incomparable learning that can only come on the job by actually functioning as a consultant. Regardless of the number of college degrees you may hold, or the type of prior work experience you may have had, it is only by practicing as a consultant under the supervision and tutelage of an experienced practitioner that you will really find out if you have the "right stuff" to succeed.

CAREER PATHS OF CONSULTANTS

In an ideal case, a consultant will join a firm at an entry-level stage and progress through the ranks until eventually rising to become a senior-level executive of the consulting firm where his/her career began.

Management consulting firms use a variety of titles for persons at different levels in the hierarchical structure of the firm. Therefore, ACME uses position descriptions when conducting research on the profession to ensure comparability of data. For our purposes we will use the ACME position descriptions to demonstrate the path a consultant's career might follow:

Research Associate—Typically full-time members of the consulting staff whose primary functions involve secondary-source research and statistical analysis; have limited or no client exposure, and typically hold a college degree.

Entry Level Consultant—Typically individuals in the first or second year of consulting, usually require close direction and supervision, and may be recipients of a graduate degree, with or without prior business experience.

Management Consultant—Typically individuals who have served as consultants beyond an entry-level apprenticeship. While not yet in a position for taking on significant project management or client-relations responsibilities, such persons have learned the fundamental disciplines of consulting and are able to work on important tasks with little direct supervision.

Senior Management Consultant—Typically individuals who are senior members of the firm who are not yet considered part of the ownership structure, but who play a significant role in the day-to-day management of engagements, have continuing contact with clients, and are expected to participate in developing solutions to client problems, writing final reports, and making client presentations.

Junior Partner or Equivalent, or Principal—Typically individuals occupying key positions in business development, practice development, client relations, and/or management of engagements.

Senior Partner or Equivalent—Typically individuals having significant management and/or administrative responsibilities and who may be expected to devote a significant portion of their time to practice development, and who share in the final responsibility for management of the firm and firm-client relationships.

Not all consultants will progress through every step of the career ladder to become a senior partner of the firm. An obvious reason is that at each successive level there are fewer positions available than there are at the lower levels. Competition to move up can be fierce, and this is especially true in those firms which have an "up-or-out" policy. In these firms professional staff members are given a certain number of years in which to be promoted to the next highest level, and if they fail to achieve the promotion in that time, they are asked to leave the firm. However, failure to advance is only one reason some people do not follow the career path.

Some people will enter the consulting arena and stay for only a short time before leaving to return to business, government, teaching, etc. Others will be recruited away to join other consulting firms, sometimes jumping two or three rungs on the career ladder by doing so. Still others will depart large firms in order to set up their own consulting entities, thereby bypassing the career ladder entirely. And some consultants will simply prefer to spend their entire career doing technical consulting work without taking on supervisory responsibilities.

COMPENSATION

Newspapers love to print stories about the "outrageous" salaries paid to consultants who, they would have you believe, have no experience or have done nothing to justify their fees. The truth of the matter is that these reports are often greatly exaggerated or leave out important details, such as the recent newspaper article which claims a new consultant had been paid in excess of $100,000, but omitted the fact that the individual had seventeen years' experience as a senior-level executive in a particular industry prior to joining the consulting firm. So, while the article was correct in calling this person a new consultant and saying that his compensation was fairly high, it was actually lower than what he had been earning in his business career. In reality, consultants can earn a comfortable living, but it is unlikely they will get rich from their efforts. According to a survey conducted by ACME,[2] the following average compensation amounts were reported as being typical for each level of consultant for all responding firms:

Position	Base Salary	Bonus/Profit Sharing	Total
Senior Partner	$156,333	$84,564	$240,897
Junior Partner	$100,879	$39,343	$140,221
Senior Consultant	$ 74,841	$17,263	$ 92,104
Management Consultant	$ 58,497	$ 8,538	$ 67,035

Position	Base Salary	Bonus/Profit Sharing	Total
Entry Level	$ 42,437	$ 4,476	$ 46,913
Research	$ 31,405	$ 3,012	$ 34,417

While these numbers may vary considerably between firms, they at least are reflective of some common practices.

HOW DO CONSULTANTS SPEND THEIR TIME?

Consultants do not spend every available moment of every day working on client assignments. They must make time for marketing, for continuing education, for managing the consulting firm, etc. Different levels of consultants within the firm will have varying responsibilities which will impact on the number of hours the individual will have available to spend on client projects. Again, ACME has collected data on the average number of hours worked per week on client engagements[3] and what consultants do with their time when they are not on an assignment.[4]

Level	Average # of Billable Hours Worked Per Week
Senior Partners	18
Junior Partners	24
Senior Management Consultants	28
Management Consultants	31
Entry Level	28
Research	25

As shown above, the higher a consultant's position in the firm, the fewer the number of billable hours he is able to devote to client projects, due to other commitments such as marketing, administration, etc.

While billable time is an important focus for insuring the firm's short-term profitability, the effective use of non-billable time can determine the firm's long-term success. The management of the firm's marketing, recruiting, training, and administrative/ financial functions will determine the firm's future viability.

DISTRIBUTION OF NON-BILLABLE TIME
(% of Non-Billable Time Spent on Each Activity)
(All Reporting Firms)

	Senior Partners	Junior Partners	Senior Consultant	Mgmt Consul	Entry Level Consul	Research Assoc
Marketing	41.9%	41.5%	32.2%	22.9%	18.1%	27.0%
Administration/ Financial Management	26.3	17.5	16.5	14.6	15.0	16.3
Employee Recruiting	4.2	5.2	3.7	3.1	2.1	3.0
Personal Professional Development	4.1	4.9	7.2	11.8	22.1	14.9
Training Others	4.1	6.3	6.7	6.0	2.7	2.2
Non-Billable Travel	3.9	3.3	4.2	4.4	2.7	0.8
Vacation/ Holiday/ Sick Time	9.6	12.7	15.6	18.2	18.6	18.2
Other	5.9	8.6	14.1	19.0	18.7	17.7
Total	100.0%	100.0%	100.0%	100.0%	100.0%	100.0%

7
CHANGE AND GLOBALIZATION

THE RATE OF CHANGE IS INCREASING

At a pace unprecedented in modern history, the way business is done is changing. Whole industries are being reshaped; military bases are closing and defense contractors are refocusing their entire operations; banks have become global financial networks; and the health care profession is no longer run by medical practitioners. Stakeholders are demanding more from corporate leaders and want a faster return on their investments, thereby shrinking the time frame of strategic planning while at the same time increasing the need for an understanding of future possibilities. Time and distance are becoming less relevant as technology and electronic commerce make the

---

Problem-Solver 7-1
COPING WITH CHANGE

The Issue

There's so much change going on. How do I cope with it?

Let's Work This Through

Change can be exciting and motivating, or anxiety-producing and debilitating. The difference lies in how you perceive change. Here are some tips to make it a positive experience:

▲ See change as a challenge rather than a threat. This is your chance to shine and demonstrate what you can do.

▲ Since change is inevitable, make a commitment to anticipate and accept change.

▲ Realize that change does not have to equate to a loss of control. You are still in charge of your life, and often facilitating change rather than waiting for it to happen can enhance your sense of control.

▲ Set up a support mechanism of trusted friends in whom you can confide when the rat race starts to get you down.

world a 24 hour per day shopping center. And knowledge—not just data or even information—that is quickly accessible has become a competitive necessity. For many consultants who are locked in to outmoded techniques, the rapidity of change may sound like a death knell.

QUANTUM CHANGE IS AFFECTING CONSULTING

As clients of consulting firms feel themselves being squeezed between increasing demands of their customers and the avalanche of change, they are passing these pressures along to their consultants. This has resulted in a number of additional factors which impact the way consulting firms operate and serve their clients. These factors include:

▲ **Clients expect faster and more measurable results and value out of consulting assignments.**

Being able to gather and carefully analyze every bit of data even remotely related to your consulting engagement, preparing a handsomely bound voluminous compilation of your recommendations which the client would slowly digest and then, getting around to implementing your recommendations may seem like a lot, but it's what clients expect these days. Clients today want *results*, they want them *fast*, and they want to be able to *measure the value* they derived as a result of bringing in a consulting firm.

Obviously, this has a major impact on the way you staff and manage engagements. Recommendations will be made based on less data, final deliverables will have to be constructed to provide measurable results, and clients will be more likely to demand that you be able to demonstrate precisely how your project provided value to the client's organization. This means that there will be more competition for experienced consultants who can diagnose problems and develop solutions with less information to go on. Your record keeping and tracking of projects will become more important as the client asks for more cost/benefit analyses. And your ability to provide comparisons between pre- and post-project operations will be tested.

▲ **Increasing global competition is creating more demand for consulting services that provide high value solutions on an international basis that are critical to the mission of the client organization.**

The fact that your clients have awakened to the possibilities of a global marketplace is a pretty good indication that their competitors have likewise realized the same opportunities. It also means that your clients are facing new competitors from other parts of the world with whom they may not be as familiar. They are going to turn to consultants for help in gaining an understanding of both the new threats and the new opportunities inherent in new markets. If you want to be the consultant they turn to, it may mean some changes in your practice.

It goes without saying that your firm's knowledge base of global best practices will be tested, it also means that you are probably going to have to be more attentive to cross-cultural and diversity issues than you may have been. Helping your clients to see where the market opportunities for their products are is only part of the solution. They may also need help in determining if there are any mechanical or physical changes which need to be made to their present products which will make the products more acceptable or easier to use in other parts of the world. In addition, your clients are going to need assistance in understanding the cultural, financial, political, etc. nuances of operating in these unfamiliar market areas. While you may not be able to personally, or even within your firm, have the capability of addressing these issues, you may still be able to help your client if you have formed strategic alliances or ventures with local consultants in the countries in which your client wishes to compete.

You may also find yourself being tested in the area of helping your client understand how his/her desire to enter the international arena does or does not support his/her organization's overall strategy. Many companies believe that because "everybody is doing it," they feel they "might as well" get involved in the global marketplace without a clear idea how or what it means in terms of their corporate vision or strategic plan. This, in turn, may mean you will need to develop a broader and more in-depth familiarity with your client's overall objectives. It would not be surprising if you found yourself helping your client to look at and come to grips with his/her own firm's strategy.

The crucial point in all of this is to make sure that the client organization derives real value from the services you provide.

▲ **New players are entering the field of consulting, thereby increasing competition.**

A.T. Kearney may be a familiar name to those involved in consulting, and possibly even to many in business generally. But names like AT&T and IBM are known to everyone. And today, AT&T and IBM (or at least divisions or groups within these organizations) have become consulting firms. And they

Problem-Solver 7-2
STAYING AHEAD

The Issue

How can I get a jump on the competition as to the next "hot" area in consulting?

Let's Work This Through

Some people may seem to have a crystal ball and be able to predict the future. If you're like most of us, however, keeping up with the present, much less eyeing the future, is hard work. For starters:

▲ Prepare a written (but not cast in stone) 3-year plan.

▲ Keep a close eye on technology and consumer buying patterns.

▲ Read about trends. Read current children's literature.

▲ Be willing to change. Look for opportunities.

▲ Eliminate the word "impossible" from your vocabulary.

Problem-Solver 7-3
PLAN ON COMPETITION

The Issue

I've got a pretty good niche carved out for myself. How do I keep competitors away?

Let's Work This Through

It's nice to say you're "customer focused," but you have also got to be aware of what your competition is doing, and how your clients view you in comparison to your competitors.

Let's face it, competition is inevitable, so you may as well plan for it. Look what happened to the U.S. automobile manufacturers when they were convinced they had the market sewn up. Without competition you will begin to grow complacent and to take your clients for granted. Competition keeps you and your firm sharp and on your toes. By preparing for competition now, you're less likely to be blindsided later.

Complacency and lack of innovation have led to the demise of more than one consulting firm. As you prepare marketing material and develop new services, consider your competitors and potential competition as carefully as you think about the needs of your clients.

do not confine their practices to a narrowly defined area such as computers or communications systems. Their business development people are knocking on the same doors and beating the same bushes as you and other established consulting organizations. Equipment manufacturers, software developers, law firms and other "non-traditional" consulting entities are crowding into the marketplace.

Companies are not the only ones seeking to cash in on the expanded market for consulting services. Downsizing, outplacements and early retirements have made large numbers of executives available to seek alternative employment, several of whom have decided to try their hands as consultants. Many of these people will not succeed as consultants, but others have and will. In some cases these new entrants to the field have made their presence felt in a big way, and since their first assignment is usually with their former employer, they are creating competition for engagements at these companies that would previously be given to established consulting firms.

Computers have also had a major impact on the way consulting is done and are another source of competition. Assignments that used to require large numbers of people to gather, tabulate and analyze data are now handled by a single consultant with a lap-top computer. Even strategic planning and process type engagements are becoming more and more dependent on computer aided assistance. The computer has enabled small consulting firms and sole practitioners to compete successfully in many cases against large firms. Today, no one is immune from competition.

▲ **Another reason for the quantum change impacting the consulting world comes from the consultants themselves who are looking for more challenging work, but at the same time want a more balanced lifestyle.**

It was long considered the norm for consultants to be on the road 50% or more of their workweek. In fact, many long term assignments would find consultants living in apartments or hotels near the client location for weeks at a time, returning home one or two weekends per month. While consulting remains a high stress, demanding profession, consultants today are seeking to claim more control over their lives, and are not as willing to totally subjugate their personal lives. They have come to realize that they can be much more effective if they have time for personal rejuvenation and to take care of family obligations. These expectations place increased demands on consulting firms to meet these needs which, in turn, means increased travel costs and the provision of other benefits. Failure to accommodate the new lifestyles desired by today's consultants could result in the departure of some staff members to more understanding employers.

At the same time consultants are asking for a richer personal life, they are seeking more challenge in their professional life. Today's consultants, because they have so much education and experience, are not enthusiastic about the prospects of "paying their dues" by conducting third party research or working on repetitive projects. They want to feel that they are growing and are looking for a variety of interesting experiences. This leads to competition inside the consulting firm as new staff members want the assignments that used to be reserved for those who had spent more years with the firm.

UNDERSTANDING CHANGE

In addition to responding to change, consultants create change. After all, consultants have been labeled change agents, and with good reason. Helping clients (and their own consulting firms) deal with change is a primary consulting responsibility. In some cases, however, it is necessary for the consultant to seek out opportunities for change and to initiate action in response to change.

To be successful, your firm and your clients must find better ways of doing what you have been doing. You must create new approaches, new products and new services. Yesterday's good enough is today's failure.

Successful consulting firms realize that change is a requirement, an integral part of business life. There are a number of principles in dealing with change that they are aware of, and that you should know. These include:

▲ Change is inevitable, and it is constant. In most cases change is gradual and hardly detectable. But even though it may be hard to notice day by day, it is there. Just as a glacier can reshape the face of the earth while moving ever so slowly, so, too, the face of business is continuously being reshaped by change. It is a mistake to assume that you will recognize major changes affecting you and your clients simply because of the scope of those changes.

Consultants should help their clients put into place mechanisms to detect and monitor changes—both within the client organization and in the world in which they operate. It is not sufficient, however, to simply realize that changes are occurring. Your clients need to know how they can respond to those changes, and this means that they need proactive plans and contingencies. Helping clients monitor, plan for and respond to change, both long-term deep-seated change and sudden or abrupt change, are crucial roles that successful consultants fill.

▲ Your competition and that of your clients are changing and improving. You cannot assume that what worked for you yesterday is going to work today, much less tomorrow. Doing what you have always done is going to cause you to fall behind because your clients are going to expect more from you. And if you don't meet their enhanced expectations, they will go looking for someone who can.

You must constantly be on the lookout for ways to improve your systems, procedures, processes, etc., and to help your clients do the same. Faster, simpler, easier to understand and work with are becoming increasingly important in a more complex world. Successful consultants continually seek ways to enhance their own services and to help their clients to improve their operations by helping them to think in terms of "systems" and integrated processes as means to achieving better results.

▲ Sometimes quantum leaps must be made to stay ahead of the competition. While most change is gradual, there are times when such things as new technology, government regulations or the sudden emergence of a new breed of competition necessitates rapid and decisive action.

It has been said that you can't cross a chasm in a series of jumps. When you identify opportunities to dramatically outdistance your competition and/or to help your clients to do so or to take advantage of unique opportunities, you simply cannot hesitate to take the leap.

▲ Dealing with or initiating change takes time and effort. Responding to change is the result of action on the part of people. This means that those people must be given the time, training and resources they need to do their jobs well.

If your people are already heavily burdened with day-to-day activities (or heaven forbid, administrivia), they are not going to have the time and energy to devote themselves to innovation and change. Successful consulting firms regularly analyze where their staff consultants are spending their time and are willing to unbundle some responsibilities as needed.

▲ Some changes are worth more than others, since neither you nor your clients can possibly handle all of the changes with which you are confronted simultaneously. In terms of risk and reward, some changes will be more valuable or important. Some changes must be addressed sequentially. Some are short-term in nature, while others may take a considerable length of time to resolve.

Successful firms focus their resources to handling those changes which will yield the greatest dividends and benefits, and which are consistent with the organization's goals, mission and strategy.

▲ Just because you are aware of changes does not mean everyone else is. Your clients may be so caught up in their own day-to-day operations that they have not taken the time to scan their environments. Your employees may not know about the new direction in which you are taking your firm.

People need to know about changes before they can respond to them. Clear and timely communication about change is crucial to the successful implementation or handling of the changes.

▲ People are usually hesitant to deal with change because they are either afraid to fail or because they don't believe they are capable of responding creatively. This is a shame because people are inherently creative, and change allows them to utilize their skills. Unfortunately, most people have also been taught to suppress their creative urgings and to seek the status - quo.

To facilitate change, you must help your clients and your staff to expand the limits of their thinking and to move beyond the "that's the way we do things around here" mentality. Help people to awaken their creativity by removing the fear of failure.

▲ Before people will embrace change, they must care about the change. Your staff and clients will not respond to or create change just because you tell them to. People want to know "what's in it for me?"

You must create an atmosphere that not only encourages, but rewards change. Review procedures, policies and work environments to make sure that they support change.

Organization change begins by changing the beliefs and attitudes of the people within the organization. An investment in training and professional development is an investment in the future of your firm.

GOING GLOBAL

Many well known, successful U.S.-headquartered consulting firms presently derive a greater percentage of the firm's revenues from projects conducted outside the U.S.

than from assignments in the U.S. There is no denying the fact that the world has become a global marketplace. And sooner or later, regardless of the size of your firm, you will find yourself considering the efficacy of having your firm enter the international arena.

Those consulting firms that have already taken the plunge point out several reasons for having done so. Some of the more obvious reasons include:

▲ Their clients force them to, especially if they serve clients who operate internationally that want their consultants to serve them wherever a need arises. Failure to be able to do so opens the door to competitors who do function globally.

▲ They can achieve greater profits by being able to leverage senior people with additional lower salaried consultants, especially in lesser developed countries.

▲ The ability to open new markets by being on-site and developing a local reputation. Plus it is a lot easier to make sales calls when you already have people in the country.

▲ To breathe new life into products and services which may have run their course or are considered "old hat" here in the States. In my experience, consulting trends and techniques usually catch on in the rest of the world three to five years after being introduced in the States.

▲ To cushion declines in the U.S. market. Historically the consulting market has been cyclical in nature, and in many other countries the market has tended to run counter-cyclically to the U.S. So when you are in a slow period here, you may be able to do quite well elsewhere.

▲ To be more competitive. Your clients and your competitors are expanding their scope of operations and causing you to do likewise if you want to keep up. There is also the advantage of becoming more aware of new opportunities to market your present offerings to a new client base, and by watching what other firms are offering, you will see other products and services you may be able to develop as practice areas for your firm.

Do not think, however, that entering the international arena is going to be easy. Interesting, challenging, potentially rewarding, yes; easy, no. You should expect to spend a few months doing research, traveling to and visiting government offices, learning the rules of the game, and generally learning what's involved and who can help you. You'll also incur expenses for site visits to different countries, and chances are if you do decide to open offices in other countries, they are not going to be immediately profitable. Plan to financially support these new operations for a period of three to five years before they begin to turn a profit.

In some ways opening offices overseas is akin to expanding into new regions of the U.S. Both take time, research, business plans, new conditions, customers and risks. However, international operations are quite different in many ways:

▲ Clients will have different tastes and needs.

▲ Licenses, rules and regulations can be quite burdensome.

▲ Shipping materials and transferring people require better planning.

▲ Pricing, payment terms and financing arrangements are much more difficult.

▲ Cultural differences must be taken into consideration.

▲ Taxes, expatriate compensation, unusual hiring laws and other human resource issues must be attended to.

TRAVEL TIPS

Let's say you've decided to check out the possibility of opening an overseas office by visiting a couple of potential locations. Here are a few tips to help you plan a successful trip:

1. Make sure you check the national calendar of each country you plan to visit to make sure you will not be trying to schedule business meetings during national or religious holidays.

2. Find out what the normal workday hours are. What time do most businesses open? Close? How long are lunch breaks.

3. Make appointments well in advance, but allow some flexibility in your schedule for contingencies. Confirm and reconfirm all appointments, travel arrangements and hotel accommodations.

4. Review your plans with a travel agent, and find out about visas, immunizations, currency restrictions and exchange rates, etc.

5. Take extra precautions to protect your passport, airline tickets, money/travelers check, jewelry and other valuables.

6. Don't forget your business cards—lots of them.

7. Find out what the weather is normally like in the countries at the time of your visits, and pack appropriately.

8. Bring all your prescription medicines, and an extra pair of eyeglasses is always worth packing.

9. Find out about local customs requirements and restrictions on what you can carry and what can be shipped.

10. Learn a few key phrases (please, thank-you, toilet/bathroom, etc.) in the language of each country you plan to visit.

KEYS TO SUCCESS FOR GLOBAL CONSULTING FIRMS

In spite of the considerable challenges that your firm will face if you decide to enter the fray of international consulting, there are a few techniques and suggestions gleaned from successful firms which may help you. These include:

▲ Developing an integrated worldwide delivery capability. Your clients want their consulting firm to meet their needs seamlessly wherever those needs arise. You must have plans and mechanisms in place as to how you are going to do so *before* the situation arises. The time to seek out and establish relationships and networks with non-U.S.-headquartered consulting firms with whom you can partner or joint-venture is now.

▲ Having a technology and communications infrastructure in place to enable worldwide coordination of resources. Both people and knowledge must be managed effectively, and to do so on a global basis requires an investment in technology and communications systems. Data must be turned into knowledge that is based on past experience so you can offer the very best of service to your clients. And that knowledge must be shared with and among your staff and your joint venture partners if it is to be effective.

▲ Organizing your firm so that it is easy to interact with your clients. Clients are much more comfortable when they know that there is one person they can turn to if they have questions or concerns about a consulting assignment. It is not up to your client to figure out who from your firm he/she should talk to. It is your responsibility to identify that person. And the client does not care about your firm's internal politics. He/She expects the person you identify as his/her contact with your firm to have the authority to get things done.

▲ Recruiting people with the appropriate skills and experience to meet the needs of your clients. In today's rapidly changing and diverse world, hiring the same kind of people you have traditionally hired may not be your best move. Take the time to assess what clients are really looking for, both in terms of industry and functional competencies. Are you in the right business? However, having the right people on staff or through relationships with other consulting firms is only part of the solution. You must be able to deploy your people quickly. Fast response time is a competitive imperative.

Problem-Solver 7-4
THE UGLY AMERICAN

The Issue

Are there certain traps I need to be aware of when negotiating internationally?

Let's Work This Through

When negotiating in cross-cultural or across different languages, proceed cautiously, especially if you are using interpreters. Other things you should pay attention to include:

▲ Don't assume that the American way is the only way.

▲ "Yes" does not necessarily mean "I agree"; it may simply mean "I hear you."

▲ Review and confirm key points of agreement.

▲ Take time to socialize, don't jump right into business.

▲ Pay attention to rank.

▲ In many cultures a final agreement is not "cast in stone" as we think it is in America.

The world may be getting smaller, but it is still a pretty big place. America is just a small piece of the world, and hard as it is for Americans to realize, the world does not revolve around us. We must become more adaptable and less egocentric to succeed in a global marketplace.

▲ Understanding and appreciating the uniqueness of different markets. The phrase "think globally and act locally" may be overused, but that does not make it any less true. Your clients expect you to help them succeed in the global marketplace. That marketplace, however, is not an amorphous, homogenous mass. Rather it is made up of many separate pieces, each of which has a certain culture, mores and ways of doing business. You and your clients must be aware of and account for these differences if you are going to succeed.

TEN GOLDEN RULES OF GLOBAL CONSULTING

1. Be aware of your own biases.

2. Be flexible in ambiguous situations.

3. Listen to and respect other points of view.

4. Be willing to take risks.

5. Be friendly.

6. Have a sense of humor.

7. Be curious.

8. Have a positive attitude.

9. Be realistic in your expectations.

10. Be honest and trustworthy.

Be aware of your own biases. We all have them, but if we aren't aware of them or refuse to admit them, our biases can get us into trouble. It is only human nature to feel more comfortable around people who are similar to us. The danger lies in thinking that those who are different from ourselves are in some way not as "good" (intelligent, sophisticated, "advanced," etc.) as we are. It is only by bringing our biases into our consciousness that we can deal with them and refute them.

Be flexible in ambiguous situations. When it is not clear as to what you should do in any given situation, it is vitally important that you remain flexible and be ready to adapt. This is especially true when you are operating in a culture other than your own. To be intransigent or convinced that "this is the way it has to be done," or that my way (or my firm's way, or my country's way) is automatically the right way is always the wrong approach.

Listen to and respect other points of view. The sooner you come to realize that you do not always have to have the last word or be right, the better off you will be and the more fun you can have. Besides, by listening to other people from other parts of the world, you might even learn something.

Be willing to take risks. Deciding to enter the global consulting arena is not for the faint of heart. Consulting is a risky proposition to begin with, and when you add the facts that you will be operating in unfamiliar cultures, in strange geopolitical areas, and dealing with unusual economic systems, a willingness to take risks is virtually manda-tory. It is also likely that you are going to be called upon to trust other people whom you may not know all that well to work on an assignment with you or to assist your

Problem-Solver 7-5
USING INTERPRETERS

The Issue

Are there any tips I should know to help me communicate better in foreign countries?

Let's Work This Through

When speaking through an interpreter:

▲ Meet the interpreter in advance so he/she can get a feel for your style.

▲ Review and define technical terms in advance.

▲ Speak slowly and clearly.

▲ It's okay to use gestures and show emotion.

▲ Watch the eyes of the person with whom you are speaking to see if your message is getting through.

▲ Ask for translation in brief bursts, not waiting for the end of a long statement.

▲ Humor and jokes rarely translate well.

▲ Use visual aids.

▲ Be careful with numbers.

▲ Confirm important issues in writing after your presentation.

client directly. Either way it is a risk you must be willing to take.

Be friendly. Let others know that you value them and appreciate their efforts. Unfortunately, the perception of "the ugly American" is all too often reinforced by the standoffish, know-it-all attitude of many U.S. consultants I have run into in other parts of the world. If you want to attract and work with consultants from or in different countries, you have to be friendly.

Have a sense of humor. An ability to laugh at yourself is perhaps the most important means of helping people to become comfortable with you and anxious to work with you. A sense of humor can get you through a lot of difficult situations. However, be careful about the type of humor you use. Jokes invariably lose something in the translation, and sarcasm may be interpreted as being a serious criticism or complaint.

Be curious. Asking questions lets people know that you are interested in their thoughts, and therefore in them. Displaying a sincere interest in their country, in their consulting philosophy, etc. can help break the ice and begin laying the groundwork for

Problem-Solver 7-6
WRITE CLEARLY

The Issue

How about written communications? Are there any tips I should know?

Let's Work This Through

When writing to overseas contacts, especially those whose English is limited, it is important to remember to:

▲ Use simple, short sentences.

▲ Stay away from slang and idioms, sarcasm and innuendoes.

▲ Repeat important or complex items several times.

▲ Check carefully for typos, ambiguities and potential misinterpretations.

closer relationships. It is also very important to keep your eyes and ears open and to stay attuned to what is going on, not only in regard to your consulting project, but on a broader societal level. Curiosity may have killed the cat, but it is the fuel of the international consultant.

Have a positive attitude. You don't want to appear cocky, but attitudes are usually contagious. And an upbeat, positive atmosphere is certainly more conducive to developing profitable relationships than giving the impression that things are bad and nothing is going to work. I found a positive attitude to be extremely important when I was consulting in the CIS countries and in Asia. By U.S. standards, the people of these countries had far less in the way of material goods than we had. They wanted to improve their lot in life. Had I not been positive and upbeat myself, my clients would have been much less likely to want to take my advice.

Be realistic in your expectations. Many U.S. consulting firms seem to have the mistaken notion that all they have to do to be successful in the international marketplace is to send one of their consulting staff members to another country, rent office space, hang out an "open for business" sign and get ready to get rich. How silly you say? Well let me hasten to tell you that I am personally aware of sexzveral firms who acted precisely in this way. And many other firms have failed to anticipate just how long it can take for a new operation or office to become profitable. Others have made the mistake of thinking that their outdated services which are no longer being sought by clients in the States will be popular elsewhere. Realistic expectations and avoiding the mistaken notion that other parts of the world are somehow "backwards" are crucial.

Be honest and trustworthy. As with the other rules listed above, the admonition to be honest and trustworthy is not limited to those who would practice international consulting. However, when dealing with other cultures where communication may not be as clear, honesty and trust take on additional importance.

In a nutshell, the best advice in dealing with all people is to be trustworthy, loyal, helpful, friendly, courteous, kind, obedient, cheerful, thrifty, brave, clean and reverent. In other words, to be successful, follow the Boy Scout oath. But you knew that, didn't you?

8
CLIENT-SAVVY CONSULTING

WHY CLIENTS HIRE CONSULTANTS

Too many consultants and consulting firms fail to pay sufficient attention to the real reasons clients seek to hire consultants. Successful firms practice **"Client-Savvy Consulting."** Here is an opportunity to get a look at what your prospective clients may be thinking.

For the past 16 years I have had the benefit of being able to listen to what clients look for when selecting and hiring consultants. One of my responsibilities at ACME was to refer consulting firms to prospective clients. It was not unusual for the association to make more than a thousand referrals a year. I therefore was able to talk with different level executives from a wide range of companies in several industries about their needs and what they expected from a consultant. This chapter includes a compilation of this information.

In addition, it will be helpful for you to know what ACME and others are telling prospective clients about how to select and work with consultants. Over the past 20 years ACME has distributed more than one million copies of its publication *How To Select And Use Management Consultants* and its predecessor booklet *How To Get The Best Results From Management Consultants*. This chapter highlights some of the recommendations being made to those who might consider hiring you.

Clients use consultants in a variety of ways depending on the particular situation and the needs of the client. Client-savvy consulting means putting yourself in the client's shoes and looking at the problem from his/her viewpoint. Doing so enables you to empathize with the client, thereby greatly enhancing the likelihood that the client will view the assignment as a success. It is worth remembering that solving the problem does not mean the assignment was successful unless the client "feels" that it was successful. Understanding where the client is "coming from" helps you to get in touch with and respond to those feelings.

Problem-Solver 8-1

COMMITTED CLIENTS

The Issue

What can I do to turn my clients from simply customers into supporters of my firm?

Let's Work This Through

Your best marketers are clients of your firm who are so delighted with the level of service you provided and the quality of the work you did that they will go out of their way to recommend your firm to their colleagues at other companies. Here are some tips to help you get there:

▲ Create and strive for a vision of perfection *from the client's point of view.*

▲ Discover and deliver what the client really *wants*, not just what he/she *says*. Find the client's sense of focus and mine it for information so you can better understand the meaning, not just hear the words.

▲ Exceed the client's expectations. Aim to deliver the client's vision plus one percent.

In my experience there are 10 major reasons clients hire consultants.

1. *To supplement the client's staff.* Often a client is not able to devote 100% of his/her time to solving one particular problem. Consultants can devote full-time attention to the problem or situation unhindered by day-to-day operating responsibilities and internal politics. By using consultants the client can avoid long-term recruitment because the consultants will leave when the assignment is completed. Occasionally consultants are even hired to fill vacant positions in the client organization on a temporary or interim basis.

2. *To gather information.* Sometimes all the client really wants from a consultant is to have the consultant gather or provide better, more complete or more reliable information. It might be market data or information about "best practices" of the client's competitors so a comparison can be made of performance issues.

3. *Developing new business contacts.* Consultants are often hired to help identify new contacts for a client that is seeking subcontractors, suppliers, joint venture or merger partners, acquisition candidates, etc. The consultant may seek out these individuals or companies, present their names to the client, assess their suitability, recommend a choice, and even serve as a facilitator in preparing and working out the deal.

4. *Providing objective opinions.* Because a consultant is expected to be independent and impartial, they are in a position to give a client an objective opinion in cases where the client management feels that its own position cannot be unbiased. In effect, the consultant's expertise is being sought to confront, assess, evaluate and confirm or correct the client's proposed course of action. There can be any number of reasons why a consultant's impartial opinion might be sought. For example, the client may feel the company lacks expertise on the issues affecting the management decision, or too many parties have vested interests to permit objective decision making to take place internally. Quite often, the client is looking for a sounding board off of whom ideas can be bounced before making important decisions.

5. *Diagnosing and solving problems.* Diagnostic skills and instruments for assessing and analyzing the causes of problems are among a consultant's principal assets. Clients, therefore, use consultants for a wide range of activities such as: assessing the company's strengths and weaknesses, identifying market and industry trends, recommending competitive positioning, etc. In some cases, a consultant is hired to conduct a diagnostic evaluation of a client's entire business operation; in other cases the consultant will be asked to focus on a narrow problem. After completing the diagnosis and making his findings known to the client, the client will decide the course of action to pursue. The client may opt not to solve the problem, or attempt to solve it without the consultant or to ask the consultant to propose appropriate alternative solutions.

6. *Developing and implementing new methods and systems.* Many clients use consultants to help modernize or upgrade their present equipment or processes. This can run the gamut from organizational systems to turnkey computer systems, from manufacturing processes to record keeping. Sometimes the consultant is asked to evaluate and recommend off-the-shelf products, and in other cases will be expected to develop customized solutions.

7. *Introducing and managing change.* Consultants are agents of change. As such, they are frequently asked in by clients who may have the technical and managerial expertise to run the firm, but are uncomfortable dealing with the organizational changes confronting the company. These changes create a lot of strain on client personnel, and as managers of change, consultants are brought in to help people understand and accept the need for change, to develop a change strategy by applying techniques for overcoming resistance to change, and to monitor progress and to adjust the approach taken by management during the change process.

8. *Training and development of client staff.* Training is often a by-product of consulting assignments as client staff is trained in the methods and techniques used by the consultant in the performance of the consulting engagement. However, training can also be used as an intervention method itself. Rather than having the consultant directly conduct the diagnostic, data-gathering and problem solving stages of an assignment, the client may prefer to hire a consultant to run training workshops to teach client staff how to address the specific subject area.

9. *To provide an "insurance" policy.* Occasionally a client will bring in a consultant as a sort of insurance policy to be able to go to his stockholders or board and say "the consultant said. . ." By doing so, if the project works, the client can take credit for bringing in the consultant who reinforced his opinions. If the project fails, the client can deflect criticism away from himself by pointing at the consultant. And sometimes a client may not even have a defined purpose in mind when inviting a consultant in. The client brings in a big name or a "guru" to have a look around in the company. If the guru finds nothing wrong, the client again can take credit for running a great operation. If the consultant does find something wrong, then the problem is fixed or the consultant gets the blame. In any case, the client feels better protected.

10. *To do the "dirty work."* Some clients are aware that the only solution to their problem is to cut back on staffing, or relocate a plant or operation, or shut down a division. And rather than handling the situation themselves, a consultant is brought in to make the announcements and to deal with the backlash.

These 10 reasons are not all inclusive, nor are they mutually exclusive as to why a client might be seeking to hire a consultant. Any given client may have any or all of these thoughts in mind. As the consultant, you should become attuned to what the client is really looking for. By becoming client-savvy, you can then determine if you are able (or willing) to live up to the client's expectations.

HOW CLIENTS ARE TOLD TO SELECT CONSULTANTS

ACME's publication *How To Select and Use Management Consultants* lists the following guidelines for clients to follow when selecting a consultant:

1. Prepare a statement outlining the scope and purpose of the assignment before you contact any management consultants. This will help you to

Problem-Solver 8-2
WHEN NOT TO USE A CONSULTANT

The Issue

Are there times when prospective clients should not hire consultants?

Let's Work This Through

Occasionally, there are situations where hiring a management consultant may not be the best course of action. These situations usually occur when the project or problem is not sufficiently defined or when management is not totally committed to the engagement. ACME advises clients to remember these four rules. Knowing them can also save you as a consultant a lot of grief:

1. Do not hire a management consultant until you have tried to develop a clear understanding of the project objectives.

2. Do not hire a management consultant unless you have full commitment from management to support the project financially and organizationally.

3. Do not hire a management consultant to run your business indefinitely. A management consultant has a professional responsibility to see that the recommendations are implemented, but it is your responsibility to decide how to implement them and with whom.

4. Do not hire a management consultant unless you are prepared to provide ongoing support during and after the project. Many management consulting assignments require client personnel to be retained and to supervise the program after implementation to ensure its success.

better define your problem and determine the kind of management consultant you need.

2. Consider the general qualifications of a number of management consultants who appear to meet your requirements. Conduct reference checks on their general reputation and then select two or three for interviews.

3. Hold preliminary discussions with each of the selected management consultants to discuss the project and their approach to it, and ask them to submit proposals.

4. Study the proposals in terms of the management consultant's understanding of the problem, the suggested approach, probable benefits, and the particular experience and ability of each management consultant to meet the requirements of the engagement. Also, consider the qualifications of the individuals who will be working on the project.

5. In some cases, it may be wise to make in-depth reference checks on those management consultants seriously being considered.

6. Review total project cost and the management consultant's fee proposal since fees are established by a variety of methods.

7. Make your final selection after carefully weighing all of the above factors.

As part of being client-savvy, you should also have some idea of the types of questions that your present clients may be asked by a prospective client who is conducting a reference check on your firm. ACME recommends the following questions:

▲ What was the nature of the work done by the consultant?

▲ Did the consulting staff assigned to the project demonstrate professional competence, objectivity and integrity?

▲ Did they work constructively with client personnel?

▲ Did one or more principals spend sufficient time supervising the work?

▲ Were the solutions complete, timely, practical and suited to the client's specific needs?

▲ Was the suggested course of action the most effective and economical from the client's point of view?

▲ Was the work accomplished within reasonable time and fee limits?

▲ What was the operating impact of the management consultant's work in the client organization?

▲ What is the overall evaluation by the client executives of the value of the management consulting engagement?

▲ Would the client retain the management consultant again?

In my experience and based on interviews with numerous consulting firms, about 75% of consulting engagements from new clients stem from the direct recommendation of a previous client. Client-savvy consultants will pay attention to the above questions and try to make sure that the quality of their work will enable their clients to answer these reference check questions.

WOOING CLIENTS

You have undoubtedly seen failed relationships where the main complaint of one or both of the parties was, "You never listen to me." Unfortunately, that same complaint is often the reason for failed consulting assignments or lost sales opportunities. Clients simply prefer to do business with those with whom they have a rapport—people they know, like and trust.

If you let your clients know you care about them and what they have to say, they will tell you exactly how to keep them happy and how to sell to them.

There is a direct correlation between how much a client talks to you and the likelihood he/she will trust you. The more they talk, the more comfortable they become. The higher the comfort level, the greater the level of trust and the stronger the bond.

Your first step in establishing a trusting, client-savvy relationship is to become a good listener. A good listener is an active and sympathetic listener who hears not just the words, but is attuned to the emotions of the speaker. A good listener gets in tune with what the client is *really* saying. So let the client or prospect do most of the talking. As the listener, you can actually control the conversation by asking questions to direct the flow of the dialogue.

Asking questions also displays an interest in the client and indicates that you want to know more about them and their needs. Non-threatening, open-ended questions can help to put the client or prospect at ease, and the answers might alert you to additional products and services you can offer.

It also helps to pay attention to body language, both yours and the client's. For your part, you must convey the certainty that you are paying attention. If the client thinks that you have lost interest, he/she will stop talking. Nod your head, maintain eye contact, smile. Make the client feel good about talking to you.

Taking notes during your conversation can make the client feel important, that his/her ideas have value. Besides, your notes can prove helpful later when you are discussing details and want to refresh your memory on some particular point.

Remember, the goal is to get to know more about the client and his/her needs. Don't immediately offer solutions to every issue brought up. Wait until you have a more complete picture and understanding. Too quick an answer can make it seem like you are trivializing the client's perceived magnitude of the problem. You must walk a fine balance between letting the client know that you can help, while not demeaning the call for help.

When courting or wooing clients, you have to be yourself. You will never develop a close relationship by pretending to be other than what or who you are. Clients do not like to be misled. You want the client to be open and honest so you can become more client-savvy. Likewise, you, too, must be open and honest with the client if the relationship is to grow.

WHAT CLIENTS LOOK FOR

After analyzing requests for referrals received from clients over the past few years, the following five criteria are what they are looking for in the consulting firm they want to hire:

1. Industry knowledge

2. Functional skills

3. Relationship management skills

4. Experience

5. Global delivery capability

Industry knowledge—With downsizing and early retirement decimating the ranks of many companies, clients are turning to consultants to bring in-depth knowledge of the client's industry to bear in addressing the problem for which a consultant is being sought. This is a change from only a few years ago when clients felt that they knew their industry and were looking for consultants with a broad range of experiences in a variety of industries to provide an overview of changing business operations.

Functional skills—In addition to industry knowledge, clients are asking that their consultants have expertise in a specialized field. It is not enough to be a generalist in the client's industry; clients also want their consultants to know the nuances and best practices of the particular functional area where the problem resides.

Relationship management skills—Clients do not want to have to guess which member of the consultant's staff they have to talk to as different issues arise. Clients expect to have one senior person from the consulting firm assigned to manage the client/consultant relationship. That relationship manager not only oversees the present project, but knows all of the other services and resources of the consulting firm and can bring them to the attention of the client to solve other problems as they are identified. The relationship manager resolves any disputes between the client organization and the consulting firm, and coordinates all contact between the two entities.

Experience—Clients don't want to be training ground for new consultants. They believe that their problem warrants the attention of experienced people. Client-savvy consultants are adept at balancing the desire of clients for senior people with the need of the consulting firm to gain experience for its new hires.

Global delivery capability—As the world becomes a single marketplace, even smaller sized client organizations envision themselves as global competitors. They want their consultants to be able to serve them wherever they are doing business, or hope to do business.

In addition to these five criteria, clients today are also asking for:

▲ **Implementation**—Rarely are written reports sufficient today to qualify a project as a success. Clients want their consultant to demonstrate the efficacy of their recommendations by participating in their implementation.

▲ **Performance based pricing**—Not only do clients want the consultant to help with implementation, but in some cases are asking the consultant to share in the financial implications of their recommendations. This "put your money where your mouth is" thinking, however, can jeopardize the objectivity of consultants by encouraging them to implement solutions which might bring about short term financial gain, but might not be best for the client over the long haul.

▲ **Understanding the needs of the client**—Clients need to believe that their needs are not only unique, but that the consultant understands their uniqueness. They don't want to feel that the consultant has preconceived or "off-the-shelf" solutions to recommend before the client even has a chance to articulate the problem.

WHAT CONSULTANTS NEED

Client-savvy consultants not only pay attention to what clients are saying today, they try to anticipate the needs of tomorrow. Here are some of the things the more successful firms are doing to respond to the needs of their present clients and to prepare for the future:

▲ **Worldwide knowledge base of best practices**—not just a database of what world-class firms are doing, but an understanding of how and why these firms do what they do. Client-savvy consultants use this knowledge to help their clients gauge their operations compared to the practices of the best companies in their industry. By understanding how these companies operate, successful consultants are able to provide their clients with more than just numbers to strive for.

▲ **Global industry teams**—an ability to put together the best possible team of industry specialists from around the world to deal with a client problem is becoming a necessity to be the consultant of a global client. In some cases this may mean that two or more consulting firms will work together to serve a single client through joint ventures and strategic alliances.

▲ **Single point of contact for each client**—as noted previously, clients want to know who to turn to at the consulting firm. Client-savvy consultants respond to this, and they also realize that assigning each major client to a relationship manager can facilitate the cross-selling of the various services of the consulting firm.

▲ **Customized solutions**—as client problems become more complex and the rate of change increases, consultants realize that what worked yesterday may not work today, and more than likely will not work tomorrow. Successful consulting firms realize that R&D expenditures represent an investment in the future.

▲ **Technology infrastructure**—keeping up with technology is an absolute must to be an effective consulting firm. But having the proper hardware, and even the latest software, is only part of the solution. Successful firms have mastered the art of "peopleware" or the integration of people with technology. Without a commitment to the timely and accurate input of data by all members of the firm's consulting staff, the hardware and software might just as well remain in their boxes.

WHAT THE CLIENT IS FEELING

To be client-savvy means not only understanding what the client wants, but getting in touch with how he feels. Remember, perceptions create reality, so your client's perceptions must be addressed if you are to be successful in consulting.

Bringing in and working with consultants is always fraught with anxiety. Understanding this and helping to reduce or control the client's level of anxiety will go a long way toward making the engagement a positive experience.

To get in touch with some of the negative emotions felt by your client, call to mind a major purchase (say buying a house) you may have made, and think of how you felt as you went through the buying process. Now add to that the fact that many people in your client's organization will be looking over their shoulders and second-guessing their decisions to bring in a consultant. No wonder they feel threatened.

By hiring a consultant, your client has placed him or herself in risk. He is turning over some of his control to an outsider, and in effect, admitting that he needs help. You need to be cognizant of your client's vulnerability and make sure that you provide prompt attention and demonstrate serious concern for his problems.

Your client wants to trust you, and it is up to you to help her overcome her insecurity by always being trustworthy. She is counting on you to help her define, as well as to solve, her problem. She needs to be reassured that you have her best interests at heart. Don't be surprised if she is somewhat skeptical. She may have been burned by a consultant before, or maybe simply heard the horror stories about unscrupulous consultants. You must make the time and effort to relieve her concerns and earn her confidence.

In dealing with clients, you must remember that the client is a person or group of persons. Your client is not a department or a company. Therefore, you must offer more than technical skills. You must demonstrate empathy—the ability to get inside your client's head and see the world through his eyes. You must become client-savvy.

HOW TO FIND OUT WHAT CLIENTS WANT

Client-savvy consulting firms know that they can achieve a competitive advantage by having a better understanding of what clients want and need than their competitors have. Garnering this understanding comes from listening to clients.

Keeping your eyes and ears open while on assignments is good advice, but it is not sufficient. Nor is sitting around in staff meetings asking, "So what do you hear in the marketplace?" Neither are market research studies conducted every few years as part of the your firm's planning efforts. To really know what clients want takes work and a systematic, structured approach.

During my years at ACME, we had several conferences and meetings during which there were many discussions and even presentations (including some by clients) about what clients want. Unfortunately, far too few consulting firms got the message—if you want to know what clients want, go out and *listen* to the clients.

Ironically, some firms hesitate to find out what their clients think because they are afraid that the client may have something negative to say about the work the consultant has done. Be assured, if the client is dissatisfied with your work, she will not hesitate to tell her colleagues at other companies about it, and maybe she will even happen to mention it to your competitors. Believe me, you are better off knowing that there is a problem so you can correct it. Burying your head in the sand and pretending everything is all right exposes another part of your anatomy which your competitors will be only too happy to kick.

It is also crucial to base new product or service development on the input from clients rather than jumping into a new service area because one of your staff consultants (or even one of your executives) thinks it will be a "hot" offering. Unless clients want or need the new service and are willing to buy it from you, it makes no sense for your firm to spend the time and money to develop it. You won't know how to proceed until

Problem-Solver 8-3
LISTENING SKILLS

The Issue

I need to know what my clients are thinking to become more client-savvy. How do I find out what's going on in their heads?

Let's Work This Through

It may sound simplistic, but the best way to find out what your clients want is to *listen* to them. Chances are they regularly tell you what they are looking for, but most people only listen with 25% efficiency. However, you can improve your listening skills. Here are 10 things you can do:

1. Listen for ideas that are of interest to you and that you feel you should know.

2. Pay attention to the content, not the delivery. Separate what is said from how it is said.

3. Don't jump to conclusions or assume that you know what the speaker is going to say.

4. Focus on the main ideas of what is being said.

5. Stay flexible and don't try to force the speaker's comments to fit a pattern already in place in your mind.

6. Let the speaker know you are paying attention by eye contact and facial expressions.

7. Eliminate or ignore distractions. Focus on what is being said.

8. Be aware of your biases so they don't get in the way of your ability to really listen to the speaker's message.

9. Don't let your mind wander. People can generally think four times faster than they can speak. Rather than becoming impatient with the slowness of the speaker, use the time to summarize what you have heard.

10. Listen between and behind the words to determine the intent as well as the content of the message.

the client has been heard from. And the more frequently you are in communication with your clients, the more valuable the advice will be.

There are several ways client-savvy consulting firms can listen to their clients. Some are more formal than others, but all can be effective. Among the more common techniques for gathering input from clients are:

▲ Attending meetings of associations to which your clients belong. There are many thousands of associations in the United States, and many thousands more worldwide. There are undoubtedly one or more associations representing the industries or functional areas in which your clients operate. These trade associations or industry groups hold meetings at which their members (your clients and prospective clients) talk about challenges facing their industry and exchange ideas as to how they can improve their operations or get more business. Such presentations and dialogues can be a virtual gold mine of opportunities for a savvy consultant. In fact, I usually recommend to my clients that they not just attend these industry meetings, but where possible, join and become active in the association so people are used to seeing them around, and are even more willing to share their needs and concerns openly with the consultant.

▲ Having senior level executives of the consulting firm visit with the client over dinner or other "outside of the office" venues. This provides an opportunity to not only ask questions as to how the present project is going, but to talk about what the client foresees for the future of his/her company. By having senior level executives involved, it demonstrates the importance you attach to the client, and may entice the client company to have some of its senior level people meet with yours.

▲ Asking focus groups of five to seven clients to come together to provide feedback on the consulting firm's plans for new services or products and ways to enhance its present offerings. The clients are asked to critique the plans from a user's point of view and to provide ideas as to how the consulting firm could best meet their needs. Clients are willing to participate because they realize the consultant wants to become more valuable to them, so it is in their own self interest to help. And client-savvy firms can, by holding focus group meetings a few times a year, get their clients to do much of the strategic planning for the firm.

▲ Bringing client executives into the consulting firm to be guest speakers or to conduct workshops for the consulting firm's professional staff. The client should recognize that you are sincerely interested in what he has to say because you want to do a better job of helping his company. It certainly has this effect, and in so doing, enhances your relationship with that client. But it also has the added benefit to your firm of helping your people to learn more about the particular industry or area of expertise of the client, thereby expanding their knowledge base. It bears remembering, however, that the client must feel that he is being invited in because you want to hear what he has to say and not that he is going to be a captive audience for your firm's sales spiel.

▲ Market research can help a consulting firm gather generic information about a large market area or demographic trends. But because consulting services are marketed to individual clients and each project is customized to meet the needs of that client, it is dangerous to attempt to draw too many conclusions from aggregated data.

▲ At the conclusion of each engagement, the project leader should sit down with the client to get the client's impressions on what went right during and with the project, what things did not go as well, and what might have been done differently or better. The discussion should cover relationship matters as well as the technical aspects of the assignment. The team leader should also debrief all the members of the team from his/her own firm, as well as from the client organization if possible. These discussions can have many benefits for the consulting firm, including ideas for improvements on future projects and the possibility of uncovering opportunities for additional projects with the present client as unresolved problems are brought to light, and by collecting and sharing information about every project throughout the consulting firm, the firm can begin to develop its own best practices database of techniques.

▲ In addition to face-to-face debriefings, some highly successful firms also require a questionnaire to be sent to each client at the conclusion of an engagement. This permits the client to evaluate the firm and to possibly be more frank and open than he would in a meeting with the project manager of the consulting firm. Another benefit of the survey format is that it can be measured more objectively than the project leader's recollections of the interview with the client.

All consulting firms claim to talk with their clients. In my experience, most of the talking is done *to* the client. And even when the client is listened to, many firms have not implemented a means for gathering and disseminating the data throughout their firm. It is not enough to merely know what clients want. Client-savvy firms know how to *use* the information.

9
LEGAL AND
ETHICAL ISSUES

THE NEED FOR ETHICS

The growth of management consulting has enticed many people to "hang out a shingle" and proclaim themselves to be in the business of consulting. Unfortunately, some of these would-be practitioners are really not competent in terms of expertise nor professional in terms of adherence to ethical standards. And it is these "rotten apples" that spoil the barrel and bring discredit to all of us who are striving to enhance the professional standing of management consultants.

There are two fundamental reasons why a profession such as consulting should have ethical standards. The first from the consultant's point of view is that high standards make the profession reputable in the eyes of clients which makes it more likely the client will turn to the professional for help with his/her problems. The second reason is that consultants deal with other people's money, lives and careers. You have a responsibility to those who have placed their trust in you.

Codes of ethics and standards of professional conduct are adopted by management consultants on a voluntary basis to demonstrate a willingness to adhere to a code of discipline above that which is mandated by law. The most frequently cited code of ethics is that of the Council of Consulting Organizations, and is the code to which members of ACME and members of the U.S. Institute of Management Consultants subscribe.

CODE OF ETHICS

The Council of Consulting Organizations, Inc., Board of Directors approved this Code of Ethics on January 8, 1991. ACME, and the Institute of Management Consultants (IMC) are technically divisions of the Council of Consulting Organizations, Inc.

Clients

1. We will serve our clients with integrity, competence and objectivity.

Problem-Solver 9-1
ETHICAL CONSIDERATIONS

The Issue

My firm does not belong to the consulting trade associations. Do I still have to follow a code of ethics?

Let's Work This Through

Even if your firm is not a member of one of the trade or professional associations that establish and enforce codes of ethics, there are certain standards to which you should aspire. These include:

▲ to place the interests of your clients ahead of your own. The client comes first.

▲ to keep knowledge about your clients confidential and to derive no special advantage as a result of your knowledge. Be wary of insider trading temptations.

▲ not to accept commissions from other suppliers in exchange for recommending their products in your consulting engagements without the client's advance knowledge.

▲ not to hold any business interest or serve as a board member of any competitor of your client without your client's knowledge.

▲ not to recruit your client's employees for positions with your firm or on behalf of another client.

▲ to inform your client of any relationships or interests that might impair your judgment.

▲ not to accept assignments beyond the scope of your competencies.

2. We will keep client information and records of client engagements confidential and will use proprietary client information only with the client's permission.

3. We will not take advantage of confidential client information for ourselves or our firms.

4. We will not allow conflicts of interest which provide a competitive advantage to one client through our use of confidential information from another client who is a direct competitor without that competitor's permission.

Engagements

1. We will accept only engagements for which we are qualified by our experience and competence.

2. We will assign staff to client engagements in accord with their experience, knowledge and expertise.

3. We will immediately acknowledge any influences on our objectivity to our clients and will offer to withdraw from a consulting engagement when our objectivity or integrity may be impaired.

Fees

1. We will agree independently and in advance on the basis for our fees and expenses and will charge fees and expenses that are reasonable, legitimate and commensurate with the services we deliver and the responsibility we accept.

2. We will disclose to our clients in advance any fees or commissions that we will receive for equipment, supplies or services we recommend to our clients.

Profession

1. We will respect the intellectual property rights of our clients, other consulting firms and sole practitioners and will not use proprietary information or methodologies without permission.

2. We will not advertise our services in a deceptive manner and will not misrepresent the consulting profession, consulting firms or sole practitioners.

3. We will report violations of this Code of Ethics.

When you get right down to it, written codes of ethics have little, if any, enforcement mechanisms. You are not going to be put in jail for violating an ethical standard, but you can be assured that the word will get out if you demonstrate that you are someone who cannot be trusted. And since consulting success is based on trust, why take chances?

LEGAL ISSUES

As a consultant you are in the business of giving advice. That advice is based on your best efforts to correctly diagnose the client's problem, to gather and analyze appropriate data, and to recommend solutions. You are involved in a high-stakes game with often a great deal of money and possibly even the future of entire corporations at risk. As such, it is not outside the realm of possibility that some party will not like the results of a consulting project and initiate legal action against you. As our society becomes

---

> ## Problem-Solver 9-2
> ## LET THE LAWYERS DO IT
>
> **The Issue**
>
> Why can't I just let my lawyers handle all the legal issues?
>
> **Let's Work This Through**
>
> Your lawyers and law firm should be a valuable resource to help keep you out of legal trouble. But, be careful that you:
>
> ▲ Don't rely on them to the point that they in effect are running your firm.
>
> ▲ Don't call them and start the clock running until after you have reviewed the document or issue in advance and have specific questions.
>
> ▲ Don't use them to draft or write letters or documents. You can save money by using them as legal editors, not composers.
>
> You don't need a law degree. In most cases common sense and adherence to the Golden Rule should be enough to keep you out of trouble. However, in today's litigious society, when in doubt, get legal advice.

ever more litigious, it is entirely likely that we will hear of more and more lawsuits against consultants as has already happened to auditors.

In prior years, consultants were able to offer the defense that they simply offered recommendations, while the actual decisions were made by client executives. With more and more responsibility for implementation being taken on by consultants, however, their potential for liability increases.

Another way consultants open themselves for liability is by making expressed or implied promises in their proposals and contracts. You want the client to hire you, but you must be careful not to promise things which you may not be able to deliver. Michael Garrett, Esq., Associate General Counsel at Coopers & Lybrand, L.L.P., has provided the following example of words and phrases which have gotten consulting firms in trouble, and gives suggested changes as well:

> *As the leading experts in the field, our firm will, in strict conformity to your urgent schedule, for fees and expenses not to exceed $_____, analyze all aspects of the problem; deliver a comprehensive report on your needs and all possible solutions; select, purchase, enhance, implement and forever debug software methodologies and*

business systems; reorganize, train and keep the same individual staff members assigned for as long as it takes to insure that all of your objectives for the project have been fully achieved employing the very highest professional standards to your complete satisfaction.

Evil Statements	Good Alternatives
Very Highest Standards	All Applicable Professional and Technical Standards
Expert; Specialized	Professional; Seasoned; Experienced
Comprehensive	Thorough
Determine; Select	Recommend; Present
Optimum Solution	Appropriate Solution
Look at All Aspects	Conduct Necessary Review
To Your Satisfaction	In Accordance with this Proposal or Agreement
Including but Not Limited to	The Following
State of the Art; Cutting Edge	The Most Current Proven Technology
Promise	Objective
Ascertain or Know Your Needs	Help You Articulate Your Needs
Best Possible	Reasonable; Adequate; Appropriate
Implement	Assist; Provide Professional Services in Connection with Implementation
Satisfy	Address
The Program Will	The Program is Designed to
Insure; Warrant; Guaranty	Provide Reasonable Assurance
Indemnify	Sympathize
Time is of the Essence	Timely
Goods or Products	Services; Deliverables

LEGAL BOOBY TRAPS

At a recent ACME meeting Attorney Garrett listed a number of other booby traps consultants can fall victim to that can lead to legal problems. Here is his list, along with some comments I would offer based on my experience:

MINDSET

▲ **Failing to perform the sniff test.**

If it smells "fishy" keep away from it. Use all of your senses to help you stay out of trouble. If you don't like the feel of it, if you don't like the sound of it, if it doesn't look right, or if it leaves a bad taste in your mouth, chances are it's going to get you into trouble.

▲ **Dropping your healthy skepticism.**

Do not assume that just because the client tells you something is true that it necessarily is true. It doesn't mean he/she is lying, it is just that perceptions can create an image of reality. If you have any doubt, check it out.

▲ **Acting as a rationalizer rather than a consultant.**

You are hired to provide objective advice and counsel, not to justify preconceived notions or actions of your client. If the client makes a mistake and gets in trouble, guess who he/she will point to and say, "He/She told me it was okay to do it."

▲ **Ignoring your subordinates.**

You cannot ignore the warnings or the actions of your staff members. On the one hand, they may be able to keep you out of trouble; on the other hand, they can get you into all sorts of trouble.

▲ **Being afraid to resign when threatened or misled.**

You must maintain your objectivity, integrity and independence to be effective. If the client can get away with misleading you or bullying you, he/she will certainly not be afraid to sue you.

▲ **Believing that it is easier to beg forgiveness later than to ask in advance.**

When your consulting project costs the client money or people their jobs because you acted without having the facts because you failed to ask for them, an "I'm sorry," will probably not suffice.

INTERNAL MATTERS

▲ **Conducting no meaningful transition to a successor consultant.**

You will undoubtedly want to carefully protect the client relationships and judicially guard the consulting techniques you have developed over the years. However, you are not going to be around forever, and the future of your firm will depend on how well you have trained those who will follow you. Not only do your successors need to learn the "hows" of what you do, but their development must also include the "whys." This means that part of your firm's training must be in legal and ethical considerations.

▲ **Delegating engagement planning too far down the line.**

You undoubtedly have a lot of demands placed on you for your time, so you have learned to delegate. But you must avoid either delegating too far down the line or having your subordinates delegate to their subordinates, who delegate to their subordinates until the engagement plan is drafted by people so far down in the organization that legal issues and ethical nuances have been lost. If you are ever brought to court, finger pointing at underlings is not a strong defense.

▲ **Permitting incomplete, flippant or CYA workpapers.**

It is well worth remembering that "if it is written down, it can be subpoenaed." Make sure your workpapers (and those of others in your firm) could stand up to courtroom scrutiny or would not embarrass you if they wound up on the pages of *The Wall Street Journal.*

▲ **Losing contact with engagements, especially troubled engagements.**

In consulting engagements, the problems you ignore are not only not likely to go away, they will more than likely jump up to bite you. You don't want your subordinates to get the impression that you are constantly looking over their shoulders, but neither can you afford to ignore or lose contact with engagements on which they are working. Successful firms devote considerable resources to develop and implement engagement tracking and reporting systems.

▲ **Failing to reserve your rights in your deliverables.**

It is not only the client who has rights under the law. You, too, have legal protection. But you must be careful to expressly reserve your rights, in writing, from the outset. This is especially true when the engagement calls for you to deliver systems or products. Questions such as: Does the client own or just license the right to use the system? Does the responsibility for the performance of the product reside with the consultant, the manufacturer or the user? How is "satisfaction" defined? These issues should be resolved and understood up front between you and the client.

HUMAN RESOURCE MATTERS

▲ **Forgetting age, gender, ethnic and other sensitive characteristics of staff.**

Your consulting practice is a business. As such, you will be expected to abide by the same personnel laws as any company. Because consulting is a travel intensive, stressful occupation, you must be extra sensitive to not make generalizations or assumptions regarding age, gender and other characteristics.

▲ **Assuming that Affirmative Action/Equal Employment Opportunity laws do not apply outside the U.S. or to partner selection and treatment.**

By and large, expatriate personnel are covered and protected by the same laws and safeguards as your staff members in the U.S. Additionally, partners do not give up their rights either. Partner selection criteria must follow the law as well.

▲ **Doubting that today's friendly CFO or loyal managers are tomorrow's panicked witnesses looking for someone else to blame.**

Just because they hired you doesn't mean they are your friends. Be discreet in what you confide to your client—it may come back to bite you. When their job is on the line, it is safe to assume that they are going to grab onto anything that can save them, even if it means throwing you to the sharks.

▲ **Believing that oral representations and personnel manual statements are not binding commitments to your staff.**

It is not at all uncommon for courts to hold that verbal commitments can have the force of law. Compliments and promises to employees can make it very difficult to terminate their employment should the need arise. And if it is in writing in your personnel manual, you had better follow it.

▲ **Trusting that your employees, independent contractors and subcontractors will not run off with your intellectual property.**

While explicit and carefully crafted contracts signed by your employees, independent contractors and subcontractors cannot prevent them from stealing your firm's intellectual property, they may at least discourage them from doing so, and will provide for legal recourse if they do run off with your material.

▲ **Hoping that mergers cancel prior obligations to employees.**

A merger will not let you off the hook. However, some firms have been able to get signed letters of understanding or revised contracts signed by their employees agreeing to vacate prior understandings in light of the merger arrangements.

▲ **Providing informal evaluations of client personnel.**

Treat every comment you make about any client as if it were going to appear on the front page of a newspaper or be used against you in a court of law. Either or both could happen.

LANGUAGE MATTERS

▲ **Writing in superlative, unattainable, undefinable and unprofessional verbiage.**

If you can't achieve it, or it can't be defined or readily measured, it doesn't belong in your proposal or contract. If you wind up in court, it is too late to say, "That's not what I meant" when the opposing counsel reads what is written.

▲ **Using formbook proposals, engagement and sub-engagement letters.**

Your firm is unique, your client is unique and every consulting assignment is different. Your proposals and reports should be tailored as well to meet the circumstances of each situation to make sure you and the client are in agreement, and to protect each of you.

▲ **Assuming that nothing is lost in translation.**

Care in translation between languages goes without saying. But also bear in mind that even though you and your client or you and your staff speak the same language, they may not hear what you think you are saying. Active listening and clear communication can keep you out of trouble.

▲ **Drafting and reviewing your own contracts.**

Always have someone else (preferably your legal counsel) review all contracts. The author knows what it is supposed to say, and therefore may have a hard time seeing mistakes or noticing ambiguities that can cause trouble later.

▲ **Bulking up your workpapers to disguise the substance of issues.**

Remember, your workpapers are subject to subpoena in the event of a lawsuit. Extraneous words or irrelevant data may increase the bulk of your product, but they can also be used against you.

▲ **Pretending everything you say and write will not come back to haunt you.**

It bears repeating, treat everything you say and write as if it were going to appear on the front page of the newspaper tomorrow morning—it just might happen.

CLIENT MATTERS

▲ **Investigating prospective clients with one eye closed.**

Love may be blind, but consulting engagements, like marriage, should be entered into only with both eyes open. Taking a bad assignment because you need the work can be very costly in the long run.

▲ **Scoping engagements with rose-colored glasses.**

Granted, you have to be competitive, but pricing and scoping an engagement with no room for any contingencies might win you the job, but put you out of business. Mr. Murphy's law (if something can go wrong, it will) should not be taken lightly.

▲ **Agreeing to whatever level of confidentiality the client proposes.**

Make sure any confidentiality agreement you are asked to sign does not so completely tie your hands that you will never be able to consult again. The client has a right to expect a certain amount of confidentiality, but you, too, have a right to earn a living. If you are an industry specialist, for example, and agree to not serve any competitor of your present client in that industry, what are you going to do next?

▲ **Beginning the engagement before the agreements are in place.**

You may want to impress the client with your fervor by getting a head start on the project, but until the contract is signed, you should not count on getting paid or on having a successful engagement.

▲ **Treating all of your clients as if they grew up in the Ozarks.**

You may have an MBA from a prestigious business school, have traveled extensively, and have lots of experience. And your client may not. But he/she still knows his/her company better than you do, and he/she signs the checks, but even if he/she didn't, talking down or being demeaning or condescending is not the way to ensure success.

▲ **Fighting fiercely over the wrong issues.**

There are some issues that you must fight for, but there are many others where it is far more judicious to give in to the client. If the issue does not jeopardize the overall success of the project, violate the law or cause you to act unethically, you must decide if it truly is worth having an argument over.

▲ **Accepting representations and sign-offs from other than their natural sources and in other than their natural forms.**

Binding contracts may be able to be written on the backs of cocktail napkins, but they are usually not. Verbal commitments or sign-offs may be held to supersede earlier signed documents, but why take the chance? A lower level member of the client's staff may have been delegated to sign on behalf of the client, but it is worth the effort on your part to check it out.

▲ **Performing desperate measures for dying clients.**

Sometimes when a client is "in trouble," you may be tempted to cut corners or do things you know you should not do, because you want to help him/her out. But stretching or violating the law or playing fast and loose with ethical considerations are not the ways to be helpful.

Consulting is filled with legal issues and ethical dilemmas. You must heed the former and resolve the latter, or be prepared to pay the consequences.

10
CONSULTING LAND MINES—AND HOW TO AVOID THEM

DON'T SHOOT YOURSELF IN THE FOOT

Consulting is fraught with opportunities for disaster. Legal issues, ethical issues, the vagaries of ever-changing clients can all contribute to the demise of your practice. But there are other traps and land mines of the consultant's own making strewn about the landscape which can be every bit as deadly. Listed here are ten of the most common self-destructive pitfalls consultants fall victim to. I have seen large firms and sole practitioners, experienced people and new entrants to the field alike make these same mistakes all too often. Perhaps if you are aware of them, you will be able to avoid them.

▲ **Wanting to Be Just Like Mike (or anybody else).**

A popular television commercial today encourages viewers to "be just like Mike" (Michael Jordan of the Chicago Bulls) by drinking a particular sports drink. Those interested in playing basketball would love to be just like Mike, so they try to emulate his "look," his style and even drink what he supposedly drinks as if doing so will make them as successful as Michael Jordan has been. Consulting firms often fall victim to the same mistaken notions.

I can't begin to count the number of consulting firm executives I have spoken to who, when asked to tell me about their firms, begin by saying, "We're just like McKinsey, only we. . . (charge less, are more involved in implementation, whatever)." My response is usually a long the lines of "Well, if you want to be just like McKinsey, McKinsey must be the best, so why should I hire you if I could hire McKinsey?" If I could have the real Michael Jordan play on my team, why would I settle for someone who just looks like him or wants to be like him?

It is much wiser from the outset to differentiate yourself and to proactively market your uniqueness rather than inviting comparisons with another firm and then having to defend your differences. To continue the basketball analogy, Shaquille O'Neal does not claim to be another Michael Jordan. He has his own unique identity. Likewise, your consulting practice should capitalize on its own strengths and develop its own image in the marketplace. And that image must be consistent in all of your supporting and marketing materials. The client should feel that he/she *wants* to hire you, not that he/she is settling for you.

▲ **Aiming at the Wrong Clients**

Every consultant would like to list *Fortune 500* companies among their clients. And every consultant seems to want to have the CEO of the client organization as his/her major point of contact. But there are only five hundred companies included in the *Fortune 500* list, while there are countless numbers of smaller companies that might make excellent candidates for your services. And as for the CEO as your target, it all depends on the nature of your practice. Look at the title or level of the people who tend to hire you or supervise your engagements, and gear your marketing efforts to their counterparts as your prospective clients.

It is also better to use a rifle approach rather than a shotgun in your marketing efforts. Focus on getting the clients you want, not on numbers of projects, especially if some of those projects are not good projects. I usually recommend that you identify 30 companies you want to have as clients and learn as much as you can about each firm and their decision makers and those who influence the decisions. These names become your prospect list.

▲ **Selling Projects Rather than Relationships**

Clients want to have confidence in their consultants, and confidence is based on the sense of having a relationship. Yet too many consultants see themselves as problem solvers. They want to get into the client organization, solve the client's problem and get back out to go in search of other problems. This attitude can turn off many prospective clients. You may think you are impressing them with your drive and zeal to get things done, but what they want is to feel that you know and care about them.

▲ **Selling What You Want to Sell Rather than What the Client Wants to Buy**

By taking the time to truly listen to the client, you can usually find out without much difficulty just what it is that he/she actually wants to buy. The end result of the project may be the same in the minds of both you and your client, but he/she may be expecting a much different approach than what you were planning to offer. Or you may realize that he/she actually has a much different problem than what he/she (and you) originally perceived. In such a case it is possible that you may not even be the right consultant for the job. It is a gross error to try to make the job fit your skills, and unless you actually do possess the required expertise, it is equally wrong to tell the client that your skills fit the job. Successful consultants know that it is always better to refer another consultant or consulting firm to the prospective client rather than accepting an engagement they cannot do well. The client will appreciate your honesty, and you stand a much better chance of getting future assignments from that client than if you were to botch a job.

▲ Misalignment of Your Firm

To be fully effective, your firm must be aligned properly. This means that your firm's culture (ownership structure, the actual value placed on team-work vs. individual success, etc.), organization (succession plans, geographical vs. practice area vs. industry lines of business reporting structures, etc.), strategy (growth plans, marketing schemes and practices, etc.) and compensation plans (pay for performance vs. pay for longevity or title, etc.) must all support one another. A firm that preaches teamwork but rewards individual performance sends contradictory messages to its professional staff. A firm organized along geographical lines or offices may find it hard to develop national promotional campaigns about a particular new service offering unless competent practitioners in the new line are available to or in each office. The successful management of a consulting firm requires continuous supervision, balancing and alignment.

▲ Putting Too Many Eggs in One Basket

It is easy to be lulled into a false sense of security by assuming that because you have a strong relationship and lots of business from a major client today, that you are set for your career. Client executives change companies, and your champion may not be around tomorrow. Companies merge and are acquired, and your client company could be next. Budget cutbacks are becoming a way of life at most corporations, and funding for your project could dry up. Therefore, you must continue marketing, even when you are fully booked. Look for other services and/or products you can add to your repertoire so you will be prepared in the event your main practice area begins to dry up or becomes more difficult to sell. A rule of thumb worth bearing in mind is to not depend on any one client for more than 50% of your revenues, or to devote more than 50% of your time to a single client.

▲ Ineffective Cost Management

Most consulting firms keep close track of their personnel costs. Successful firms also carefully control non-people costs. For example, it is easy to fall victim to wanting to have very attractive offices and a prestigious address. But if your clients rarely, if ever, visit your offices, how glamorous must they really be? If most of your staff spends most of their time on-site at the client's location, do they all need to have private offices at your firm? It pays to review all of your leases (office space, equipment, etc.) to seek less costly alternatives and to renegotiate them if based on market rate declines. And you may also find you can save money by outsourcing activities such as research/data collection, bookkeeping, legal, etc. rather than retaining staff to handle them.

▲ Inadequate Infrastructure

You need to have the right tools, as well as the right people, to have a successful consulting practice. You must be able to gather and process data and turn it into useful and useable information for your clients and for your firm. And you must develop a knowledge base of your firm's clients, projects, best practices and skills and experiences of your consultants. All of this means that consulting firms are going to have to spend a considerable amount of money on new technology. No longer is it the case that the entire assets of a consulting firm ride up and down on the elevator each day. More and more of a firm's earnings are going toward the purchase of computers and telecommunications equipment and on the development and maintenance of systems.

▲ People Problems

Notwithstanding the increasing amount of money being spent on R&D and technology, consulting is still basically a people business. Your firm will succeed or fail in large measure based on how well you resolve internal personnel issues including training, career pathing, compensation and making sure you hire or partner with people who can actually do the work. Too many consultants, and even consulting firm executives, tend to think of firm management (if they think of it at all other than as an afterthought) as a burden. Chances are you went into consulting because you wanted to consult rather than become a manager. However, as your firm grows, you will need to spend more and more of your time on firm administrative issues, including (perhaps especially) personnel related matters. To diminish the importance of firm administration is to diminish your firm's potential for success if not survival.

▲ Failure to Practice "Values Driven Consulting"

In my opinion, if there is one overriding factor that has contributed to the success of a select number of prestigious firms, it lies in the firm's adherence to a set of values. I use the term "values" to mean the beliefs that drive the firm. These beliefs/values must be clearly articulated by the firm's CEO, and include: leadership, teamwork, management styles, creation of a learning environment, and most importantly, integrity and ethics. In a values driven firm, staff members are evaluated not just on performance, but also on their adherence to the firm's values. You cannot simply pay lip service to values. They must be clearly articulated to and ingrained in your staff. Your clients, too, must be made aware of your firm's values, and be convinced that they are adhered to. If you are not driven by values, maybe you need to reconsider why you are in consulting to begin with.

THE BIGGEST PITFALL

As consultants we are by nature givers rather than receivers. We want to help our clients succeed. We want to teach them new approaches, and assist them in making good decisions. We want to be needed. And so it is easy to fall into the trap of believing that we are indispensable. We abandon our identities and our families for the sake of being available to our clients. We can lose ourselves if we're not careful.

To outsiders, consulting can seem an exciting profession. We get to travel extensively. We have a variety of work experiences. We don't appear to have a boss, and we seem to be able to set our own schedules. To those of us on the inside, we know that consulting can be emotionally and physically draining on the one hand, and an adrenaline-filled pressure cooker on the other. The ability to manage the stress related with consulting is a key component to being a successful consultant. There are several good books and articles available on the subject of stress management, so I will not attempt to provide a treatise at this point. However, there are a few keys that I have found to be helpful in boosting my self confidence and in turn, to better control stress. These keys are:

1. Think about how you would like to be remembered in your eulogy; decide to become that kind of person, keep that image in mind, and act as if you were that kind of person.

2. Give yourself a daily pep talk to help develop the habit of thinking about yourself positively.

3. Make a list of successes you have had in the past; keep this list in a notebook, and review and update the list frequently.

4. Avoid negative influences and negative people who pull you down.

5. Get out of your comfort (or lazy) zone by daring to do something you fear doing.

6. Do the best you can in any situation, and don't fool yourself into thinking you have to be perfect—you can't.

7. Forgive yourself for making mistakes, and appreciate your accomplishments—treat yourself as you would treat your closest friend.

8. Have faith in your own judgment and in your ability to make good decisions.

9. Learn to say NO to demands that drain your time and your energy.

10. ACT, achievements are the result of doing, not dreaming—actively strive to become the person you want to be.

To truly succeed in consulting, you have to look at more than personal financial achievements and client satisfaction surveys. You have to be able to look at yourself and realize that, when all is said and done, only you can define success for yourself.

Appendices

RESOURCES

ACME—The Association of Management Consulting Firms. 521 Fifth Avenue, New York, NY 10169. (212) 697-9693. Founded in 1929, ACME is the oldest of the consulting associations. Conducts research on the profession. Provides prospective clients with referrals. Membership directory available.

American Association of Healthcare Consultants (AAHC). 11208 Waples Mill Road, Suite 109, Fairfax, VA 22030. (703) 691-2242. AAHC has both firm and individual members. Credentials qualified consultants. Provides referrals. Membership directory available.

Association of Executive Search Consultants (AESC). 500 Fifth Avenue, New York, NY 10110. (212) 398-9556. AESC represents executive search firms that operate on a retainer basis (as opposed to contingency basis).

Kennedy Publications, Templeton Road, Fitzwilliam, NH 03447. (603) 585-3101. Publishes *Consultants News* (CN) and *Executive Recruiter News* (ERN). Produces *The Directory of Management Consultants, The Directory of Executive Recruiters, The Directory of Outplacement Firms.* Has a bookstore of consulting related books.

The Institute of Management Consultants (IMC). 521 Fifth Avenue, New York, NY 10169. (212) 697-8262. IMC is a professional association and administers the Certified Management Consultant designation for qualified practitioners. Provides referrals. Membership directory available. Management Consulting: A Workshop for Professionals.

REFERENCE MATERIALS

Survey of Key Management Information (U.S. and European editions) published by ACME—The Association of Management Consulting Firms. (212) 697-9693.

How To Select and Use Management Consultants published by ACME—The Association of Management Consulting Firms. (212) 697-9693.

The Journal of Management Consulting published by The Journal of Management Consulting, Inc. (415) 342-1954.

FOOTNOTES

CHAPTER 1

   i   ACME 1996 Survey of United States Key Management Information ©1996, Council of Consulting Organizations, Inc., p. 18.

  ii   Ibid, p. 18.

 iii   Kennedy Publications, Templeton Road, Fitzwilliam, NH 03744.

 iv   Consultants News, July/August, 1996, p. 2, Kennedy Publications, Templeton Road, Fitzwilliam, NH 03744.

  v   ACME 1996 Survey of United States Key Management Information ©1996 Council of Consulting Organizations, Inc., p. 32.

 vi   Press Release, April 9, 1996 by ACME.

CHAPTER 3

   i   ACME 1996 Survey of United States Key Management Information ©1996, Council of Consulting Organizations, Inc., p. 54.

  ii   Ibid, p. 17.

 iii   Ibid, p. 55.

 iv   Ibid, p. 43.

  v   Ibid, p. 44.

 vi   Outlook, ©1990, Ernst & Young, p. 1.

CHAPTER 6

   i   Consultants News, Kennedy Publications, Templeton Road, Fitzwilliam, NH 03477.

  ii   1995 ACME Survey of U.S. Key Management Information ©1995, Council of Consulting Organizations, Inc., New York, NY, p. 70.

 iii   Ibid, p. 47

 iv   Ibid, p. 48.

Notes

Notes

Notes

Notes

Notes

Notes

Notes